Microsoft®
PowerPoint® 2016

by Alec Fehl, Asheville-Buncombe Technical Community College

LEVEL 1

LABYRINTH
LEARNING™

Microsoft PowerPoint 2016: Level 1

Copyright © 2017 by Labyrinth Learning

LABYRINTH
LEARNING™

Labyrinth Learning
2560 9th Street, Suite 320
Berkeley, California 94710
800.522.9746
On the web at lablearning.com

Product Manager:
Jason Favro

Development Manager:
Laura Popelka

Senior Editor:
Alexandra Mummery

Junior Editor:
Alexandria Henderson

Assessment and Multimedia Content Development:
Ben Linford, Judy Mardar, Andrew Vaughnley

Production Manager:
Debra Grose

Compositor:
Happenstance Type-O-Rama

Indexer:
Valerie Perry

Interior Design:
Debra Grose

Cover Design:
Mick Koller

ebook only ITEM: 1-59136-860-X
ISBN-13: 978-159136-860-1

ebook with printed textbook ITEM: 1-59136-861-8
ISBN-13: 978-159136-861-8

Manufactured in the United States of America

GPP 10 9 8 7 6 5 4 3 2

Table of Contents

PowerPoint 2016 Chapter 4:
Adding Multimedia to Presentations

Preface

This textbook is part of our brand-new approach to learning for introductory computer courses. We've kept the best elements of our proven instructional design and added powerful, interactive elements and assessments that offer enormous potential to engage learners in a new way. We're delighted with the results, and we hope that learners and educators are, too!

Why Did We Write This Content?

In today's digital world, knowing how to use the most common software applications is critical, and those who don't are left behind. Our goal is to simplify the entire learning experience and help every student develop the practical, real-world skills needed to be successful at work and in school. Using a combination of text, videos, interactive elements, and assessments, we begin with fundamental concepts and take learners through a systematic progression of exercises to reach mastery.

What Key Themes Did We Follow?

We had conversations with dozens of educators at community colleges, vocational schools, and other learning environments in preparation for this textbook. We listened and have adapted our learning solution to match the needs of a rapidly changing world, keeping the following common themes in mind:

Keep it about skills. Our content focus is on critical, job-ready topics and tasks, with a relentless focus on practical, real-world skills and common sense as well as step-by-step instruction to ensure that learners stay engaged from the first chapter forward. We've retained our proven method of progressively moving learners through increasingly independent exercises to ensure mastery—an approach that has been successfully developing skills for more than 20 years.

Keep it simple. Our integrated solutions create a seamless and engaging experience built on a uniquely dynamic instructional design that brings clarity to even the most challenging topics. We've focused our content on the things that matter most and have presented it in the easiest way for today's learners to absorb it. Concise chunks of text are combined with visually engaging and interactive elements to increase understanding for all types of learners.

Keep it relevant. Fresh, original, and constantly evolving content helps educators keep pace with today's student and work environments. We have reviewed every topic for relevancy and have updated it where needed to offer realistic examples and projects for learners.

How Do I Use This Book?

We understand that we are in a time of transition and that some students will still appreciate a print textbook to support their learning. Our comprehensive learning solution consists of a groundbreaking interactive ebook for primary content delivery and our easy-to-use eLab course management tool for assessment. We want to help students as they transition to a digital solution. Our interactive ebook contains learning content delivered in ways that will engage learners. Students can utilize a print text supplement in conjunction with the ebook that provides all the textual elements from the ebook in a full-color, spiral-bound print format.

Our eLab platform provides additional learning content such as overviews for each chapter, automatically graded projects and other assessments that accurately assess student skills, and clear feedback and analytics on student actions.

Included with Your Textbook Purchase

▶ *Interactive ebook*: A dynamic, engaging, and truly interactive textbook that includes elements such as videos, self-assessments, slide shows, and other interactive features. Highlighting, taking notes, and searching for content is easy.

▶ *eLab Course Management System*: A robust tool for accurate assessment, tracking of learner activity, and automated grading that includes a comprehensive set of instructor resources. eLab can be fully integrated with your LMS, making course management even easier.

▶ *Instructor resources*: This course is also supported on the Labyrinth website with a comprehensive instructor support package that includes detailed lesson plans, PowerPoint presentations, a course syllabus, test banks, additional exercises, and more.

▶ *Learning Resource Center*: The exercise files that accompany this textbook can be found within eLab and on the Learning Resource Center, which may be accessed from the ebook or online at **www.labyrinthelab.com/lrc**.

▶ *Overview chapter content*: The "Overview Chapter ISM" folder in the Instructor Support Materials package and the "Overview Chapter Files" folder in the Student Exercise File download include the helpful "Introducing Microsoft Office and Using Common Features" chapter. In addition to providing a discussion of the various Office versions, this chapter introduces a selection of features common throughout the Office applications. **We recommend that students complete this "overview" chapter first.**

We're excited to share this innovative, new approach with you, and we'd love you to share your experience with us at www.lablearning.com/share.

Display Settings

Multiple factors, including screen resolution, monitor size, and window size, can affect the appearance of the Microsoft Ribbon and its buttons. In this textbook, screen captures were taken at the native (recommended) screen resolutions in Office 2016 running Windows 10, with ClearType enabled.

Visual Conventions

This book uses visual and typographic cues to guide students through the lessons. Some of these cues are described below.

Cue Name	What It Does
`Type this text`	Text you type at the keyboard is printed in this typeface.
Action words	The important action words in exercise steps are presented in boldface.
Ribbon	Glossary terms are highlighted with a light gray background.
Note! Tip! Warning!	Tips, notes, and warnings are called out with special icons.
(!)	Videos and WebSims that are a required part of this course are indicated by this icon.
Command→Command→ Command→Command	Commands to execute from the Ribbon are presented like this: Ribbon Tab→Command Group→Command→Subcommand.
≡ **Design →Themes→Themes** [Aa]	These notes present shortcut steps for executing certain tasks.

Acknowledgements

Many individuals contribute to the development and completion of a textbook. This book has benefited significantly from the feedback and suggestions of the following reviewers:

Pam Silvers, *Asheville-Buncombe Technical Community College*

Ramiro Villareal, *Brookhaven College*

Teresa Loftis, *Inland Career Education Center*

Kim Pigeon, *Northeast Wisconsin Technical College*

Lynne Kemp, *North Country Community College*

Tom Martin, *Shasta College*

Karen LuPlant, *Hennepin Technical College*

Kay Gerken, *College of DuPage*

Colleen Kennedy, *Spokane Community College*

1 Creating and Delivering a Presentation

In this chapter, you will learn to create and display a basic PowerPoint presentation consisting of multiple slides and bulleted text. You don't have to be a graphic designer to create an eye-catching presentation, as PowerPoint includes many visually appealing themes that are preformatted with fonts, colors, and supporting imagery. It is important for readability to create a visual hierarchy of text, such as headings and associated bullet points—and PowerPoint makes this easy.

LEARNING OBJECTIVES

▶ Create a new presentation

▶ Add text to slides

▶ Apply themes

▶ Add slides

▶ Control the indent of bulleted text

▶ Navigate a slide show

📂 Project: Creating a Presentation

As an employee of iJams, an online music distribution company, you have been asked to make a presentation about the company at the JamWorks trade show. Your goal is to introduce iJams to trade show attendees and entice them with a promotional offer. You decide to use PowerPoint to develop and deliver your presentation because it is easy to learn and integrates seamlessly with other Microsoft Office applications.

Getting Started with PowerPoint

PowerPoint is an intuitive, powerful presentation graphics program that enables you to create dynamic, multimedia presentations for a variety of functions. Whether you are developing a one-on-one presentation for your manager or a sophisticated presentation for a large group, PowerPoint provides the tools to make your presentation a success. PowerPoint allows you to project your presentation in many ways. Most presentations are delivered via a computer projection display attached to a desktop or notebook computer. There are also other ways to deliver presentations. For example, you can deliver a presentation as an online broadcast over the Internet or save it as a video to be emailed or distributed on a CD or USB drive.

PowerPoint provides easy-to-use tools that let you concentrate on your presentation's content instead of focusing on the design details. Using PowerPoint's built-in document themes, you can rapidly create highly effective professional presentations.

DEVELOP YOUR SKILLS: P1-D1

In this exercise, you will create a new, blank presentation.

1. Click **Start**.
2. Type **Po** and then choose **PowerPoint 2016** from the list of suggestions.
3. Click the **Blank Presentation** template on the PowerPoint Start screen.

   A new, blank presentation appears. You will develop it throughout this chapter.

Navigating the PowerPoint Window

The PowerPoint program window, like other Microsoft Office programs, groups commands on the Ribbon. While the Ribbon and its commands are similar to those found in other Office programs, there are several icons and commands at the bottom of the PowerPoint window unique to the program.

 View the video "The PowerPoint Window."

Inserting Text

PowerPoint slides have placeholders set up for you to type in. For example, the title slide currently visible on the screen has placeholders for a title and subtitle. You click in the desired placeholder to enter text on a slide. For example, to enter the title on a slide, you click in the title placeholder and then type the text. Do not press Enter; the placeholders are already formatted with Word Wrap. The placeholders are also already formatted with font and paragraph settings to make a cohesive presentation. As you will see shortly, it's easy to make changes to the slide formatting by applying a theme.

DEVELOP YOUR SKILLS: P1-D2

In this exercise, you will enter a title and subtitle for the presentation.

Before You Begin: *Be sure to visit the Learning Resource Center at labyrinthelab.com/lrc to retrieve the exercise files for this course before beginning this exercise.*

1. Choose **File→Save As** and navigate to your **PowerPoint Chapter 1** folder.
2. Name the file **P1-D2-iJams**.
3. Click the **Save** button at the bottom of the dialog box.
4. Follow these steps to add a title and subtitle:

Ⓐ Click once on **Click to Add Title** and then type the title shown here.

Ⓑ Click once on **Click to Add Subtitle** and then type this subtitle.

PowerPoint enters the titles. At this point, you have a title slide, but it looks rather plain. This is about to change.

5. Press Ctrl + S to save the presentation and leave it open; you will modify it throughout this chapter.

Using Document Themes

You can use PowerPoint's built-in document themes, which provide a ready-made backdrop for your presentations, to easily format all slides in a presentation. When you use a document theme, your presentation automatically includes an attractive color scheme, consistent font style and size, and bulleted lists to synchronize with the presentation's design and style. Document themes also position placeholders on slides for titles, text, bulleted lists, graphics, and other objects. By using document themes, you can focus on content by simply filling in the blanks as you create the presentation. You access document themes from the Themes group on the Design tab.

Choosing a Theme

More than 30 document themes are included with PowerPoint. Additionally, each theme has four variations. A theme variation uses different colors and sometimes a different background. PowerPoint automatically downloads additional themes and adds them to the Themes gallery on the Ribbon if your computer is connected to the Internet. Match the theme to the type of presentation you are giving. Keep the design appropriate to the function and the audience.

 View the video "PowerPoint Document Themes."

Finding Additional Themes

New themes are sent to Microsoft daily, so if you just can't find the right one, browse the Microsoft Office Online website for new themes. You can also search for new themes from the PowerPoint Start screen.

DEVELOP YOUR SKILLS: P1-D3

In this exercise, you will choose a document theme and apply it to the presentation.

1. Choose **File→Save As** and save your file as **P1-D3-iJams**.

2. Follow these steps to choose a theme for the presentation:

   Depending on your monitor resolution, you may see a different number of thumbnails in the Themes group.

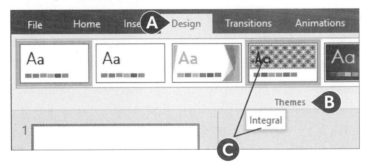

Ⓐ Click the **Design** tab.

Ⓑ Locate the **Themes** command group.

Ⓒ Point over (don't click) the fourth theme from the left and notice that the theme's name appears as a ToolTip.

Note that your fourth theme may not match the one in the figure.

PowerPoint displays a Live Preview of the theme on your title slide. This gives you a good idea of the theme's overall design. Notice that the fonts and locations have changed for the title and subtitle. A different theme can radically redesign your presentation.

3. Point over (don't click) several more theme thumbnails.

You see a Live Preview of each theme on the actual slide. The themes visible on the Ribbon are just a small portion of those available, however.

4. Follow these steps to choose a theme:

Ⓐ Choose **Design→Themes→More** ⬇.

Ⓑ Point to preview the **Organic** theme and notice the ToolTip. (The default themes are listed in alphabetical order.)

Ⓒ Point (don't click) to preview the **Wisp** theme.

Ⓓ Point to the **Ion Boardroom** theme and click once to apply it.

PowerPoint applies the theme to your presentation.

5. Save the presentation and leave it open for the next exercise.

Choosing Slide Sizes

By default, PowerPoint creates slides for widescreen format with a 16:9 ratio. This maximizes the use of space on the slide by taking advantage of the widescreen format on most modern computers. In fact, many of the new PowerPoint themes were designed specifically for widescreen use. You can easily switch to standard format (4:3) from the Ribbon if you need a narrower slide or have a non-widescreen computer monitor.

 View the video "Changing the Slide Size/Aspect Ratio."

≡ Design→Customize→Slide Size ▢

DEVELOP YOUR SKILLS: P1-D4

In this exercise, you will experiment with slide sizes and choose a document theme variation.

1. Save your file as **P1-D4-iJams**.

2. Display the **Design** tab and then follow these steps to change the slide size:

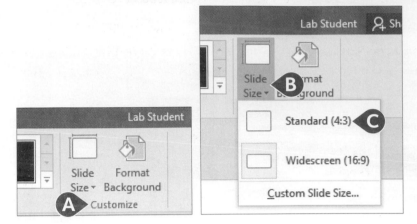

   Ⓐ Locate the Customize command group.

   Ⓑ Click the **Slide Size** menu button ▼.

   Ⓒ Click **Standard (4:3)**.

   The slide is resized, and the slide title shifts to wrap across two lines.

3. Choose **Design**→**Customize**→**Slide Size**→**Widescreen (16:9)** to return the slide to widescreen format.

4. Locate the **Design**→**Variants** group on the Ribbon.

5. Point to several theme variations to view the Live Preview on the slide.

6. Click the second variation (with the green background) to apply it.

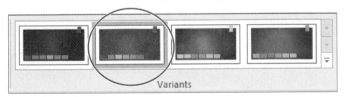

7. Save the presentation and leave it open for the next exercise.

Creating a Basic Presentation

There is more to creating a presentation than placing one slide after another. Choosing the appropriate slide layout, just like choosing the appropriate design, will influence how well your audience understands your message. Use the following guidelines when choosing your slide design and layout:

- **Know your audience:** Will you be speaking to accountants or artists?
- **Know your purpose:** Are you introducing a product or giving a report?
- **Know your expectations:** When the last word of this presentation has been given, how do you want your audience to respond to your facts? Are you looking for approval for a project or customers for a product?

Adding Slides

You can add slides to a presentation from the Ribbon or by right-clicking with the mouse. PowerPoint always places the new slide after the currently selected slide.

The Slides panel displays thumbnails of your presentation while you work in the Normal view. The Slide Sorter view, like the Slides panel, also displays thumbnails of your slides. This view can be useful when there are more slides than can fit in the Slides panel display.

≡ Home→Slides→New Slide | Right-click a slide in the Slides panel→New Slide

---

DEVELOP YOUR SKILLS: P1-D5

In this exercise, you will add a new slide to the presentation and then enter content.

1. Save your file as **P1-D5-iJams**.
2. Choose **Home→Slides→New Slide** .

   PowerPoint adds a new slide to the presentation immediately after the title slide.

3. Click once in the title placeholder and then type **Our Services** as the title.
4. Click once on the **Click to Add Text** placeholder and then type the following list, tapping ⎡Enter⎤ after each list item except the last one:
   - **CD duplication on demand** ⎡Enter⎤
   - **Jewel-case-insert printing** ⎡Enter⎤
   - **Full-service online sales** ⎡Enter⎤
   - **Downloadable MP3 distribution**

   PowerPoint adds a bullet in front of each line.

5. Save the presentation and leave it open for the next exercise.

Duplicating a Slide

Sometimes it is more efficient to duplicate a slide and then edit it rather than to begin a new slide from scratch. Slides can be duplicated via the Slides panel.

≡ One slide: Right-click the slide in the Slides panel→Duplicate Slide

≡ Multiple slides: Select the slides, right-click one in the Slides panel→Duplicate Slide

Bulleted Lists

You can effortlessly create bulleted lists to outline the thrust of your presentation. The bulleted list layout is an outline of nine levels. A different indentation is used for each level. When you use a document theme, each paragraph is automatically formatted as a bulleted list. The format includes a bullet style, indentation level, font type, and font size for each bulleted paragraph.

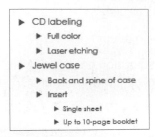

≡ Home→Paragraph→Bullets ⊞

List Levels

Indenting a bullet is referred to as demoting a bullet, or increasing the list level. Typically, a main bullet point has one or more sub-bullets. These sub-bullets, which are smaller than the main bullet, are created by increasing the list level. When a list level is increased, the bullets are indented toward the right. Conversely, decreasing a bullet's indent by moving it more toward the left and increasing the bullet size is referred to as promoting a bullet, or decreasing the list level. PowerPoint supports a main bullet and up to eight levels of sub-bullets.

≡ Promote: Home→Paragraph→Decrease List Level ⊡ | Shift + Tab

≡ Demote: Home→Paragraph→Increase List Level ⊡ | Tab

DEVELOP YOUR SKILLS: P1-D6

In this exercise, you will create a new slide and then enter information into a multilevel bulleted list.

1. Save your file as **P1-D6-iJams**.
2. Choose **Home→Slides→New Slide** ⊡.

   PowerPoint creates a new slide after the current slide.
3. Click in the title placeholder and type **Packaging Options**.
4. Click once in the text placeholder, type **CD labeling**, and then tap Enter.

   PowerPoint formats the new blank paragraph with the same large bullet. Paragraph formats are carried to new paragraphs when you tap the Enter key.
5. Tap Tab.

   PowerPoint indents the paragraph. It also introduces a new, slightly smaller style for the level-2 paragraph.
6. Type **Full color**.

   PowerPoint formats the paragraph in a smaller font, too.
7. Tap Enter.

   PowerPoint maintains the same level-2 formatting for the next paragraph.

8. Type **Laser etching** and then tap Enter.

9. While holding down Shift, tap Tab once.

PowerPoint promotes the new paragraph back to the level-1 style, which is the level of the first paragraph on the slide.

Manipulate Heading Levels

You can also adjust the level after you have typed a paragraph.

10. Type these lines, tapping Enter after each list item except the last one:
    • **Jewel case** Enter
    • **Back and spine of case**

11. Follow these steps to indent the last bullet:

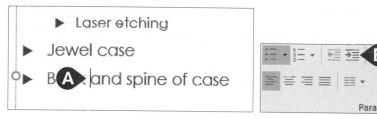

(A) Click once anywhere within the paragraph to be indented.

(B) Choose **Home→Paragraph→Increase List Level**.

PowerPoint indents the paragraph and changes the bullet style. Demoting a paragraph makes it subordinate to the preceding paragraph.

12. Click the **Home→Paragraph→Increase List Level** button three more times.

The bullet and font sizes change with each level increase. These formats are determined by the Ion Boardroom theme, on which the presentation is based.

13. Click **Home→Paragraph→Decrease List Level** three times until the bullet reaches the second indentation.

With each promotion, the bullet style changes.

Indent Multiple Bullets

14. Click once at the end of the last paragraph and then tap Enter.

15. Type these new lines, tapping Enter after each list item except the last one:
    • **Insert** Enter
    • **Single sheet** Enter
    • **Up to 10-page booklet**

16. Follow these steps to select the last two paragraphs for your next command:

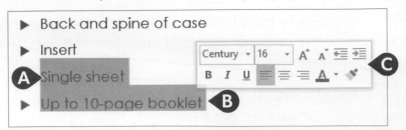

   Ⓐ Point at the beginning of *Single sheet*, taking care that a four-pointed arrow is not visible.

   Ⓑ Drag down and right to select (highlight) to the end of the last paragraph; release the mouse button.

   Ⓒ Ignore the Mini toolbar that appears. Take care not to click anywhere else on the slide before you perform the next step.

17. Choose **Home→Paragraph→Increase List Level** 📧.

PowerPoint indents the two selected paragraphs.

18. Click anywhere outside the border to deselect the text. Your slide should match the following illustration.

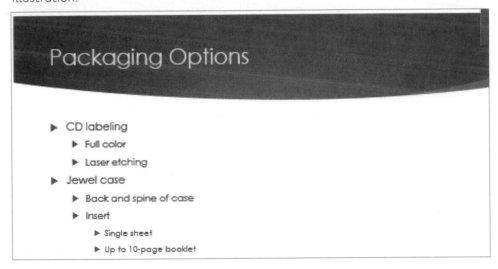

19. Save the presentation and leave it open for the next exercise.

Choosing the Slide Layout

A slide layout is named for the type of data it will contain. For example, the Title layout needs only a title and subtitle. The Content layout will hold other information on the slide, so it has a title and a bulleted list for points. Likewise, the Content with Caption layout is divided into three sections: title, text to one side, and an area for clip art or additional text. The slide layout organizes the information you put into the presentation by giving it a place on the slide. The new layout is applied to all selected slides. There are nine standard layouts, but many themes offer additional layouts.

≡ Home→Slides→Layout 🔲 | Right-click a slide in the Slides panel

Aligning Text

PowerPoint automatically aligns text to the left, right, or center depending on the theme. However, you may want to override the alignment at times to create a different look for a slide.

≡ Home→Paragraph→click an alignment button

The default formatting for this slide is left-aligned text.

The text has been centered and bullets removed for a different look.

DEVELOP YOUR SKILLS: P1-D7

In this exercise, you will add a new slide and then change its layout.

1. Save your file as **P1-D7-iJams**.
2. If necessary, select the **Packaging Options** slide from the Slides panel on the left side of your screen.
3. Choose **Home→Slides→New Slide** .

   PowerPoint adds another slide to the end of the presentation. Like the previous two slides, this one is set up to display a bulleted list.

4. Follow these steps to choose a new layout for the slide:

(A) Choose **Home→Slides→Layout menu button ▼**.

(B) Choose the **Section Header** slide layout.

PowerPoint applies the new layout. Now there are two placeholders, for a title and subtext.

5. Enter the following text:
- Title: **Questions?**
- Text: **End of our brief presentation**

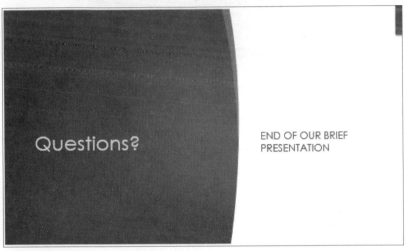

6. Click the dashed border of the text box to select it.

7. Choose **Home→Paragraph→Center** ☰.

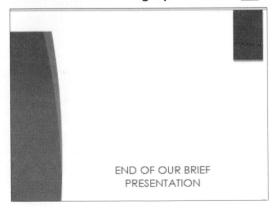

8. Save the presentation and leave it open for the next exercise.

Delivering the Slide Show

The slides are created, and the presentation is complete. The first phase of the presentation development is over. The next phase, delivering the presentation, is just beginning. Before you stand in front of an audience, familiarize yourself with the following tips:

> ☰ Start slide show: Slide Show→Start Slide Show→From Beginning 🖥 *or* From Current Slide 🖥

> ☰ End slide show: Tap [Esc] *or* click the window until the slide show ends

📖 Delivery Tips

It is not only what you say but how you say it that makes the difference between an engaging presentation and an unsuccessful one. Lead your audience. Help them to focus on your presentation's message, not on you as the presenter. Use the following *PEER* guidelines to deliver an effective presentation:

- ▶ **Pace:** Maintain a moderate pace. Speaking too fast will exhaust your audience, and speaking too slowly may put them to sleep. Carry your audience with you as you talk.

- ▶ **Emphasis:** Pause for emphasis. As you present, use a brief pause to emphasize your point. This pause will give the audience time to absorb your message.

- ▶ **Eye contact:** Address your audience. Always face your audience while speaking. A common mistake is to speak while walking or facing the projection screen. Don't waste all the work you have done in the presentation by losing your audience's interest now. If you are speaking from a lectern or desk, resist the temptation to lean on it. Stand tall, make eye contact, and look directly at your audience.

- ▶ **Relax:** You are enthusiastic and want to convey that tone to the audience. However, when you speak, avoid fast movement, pacing, and rushed talking. Your audience will be drawn to your movements and miss the point. Remember that the audience is listening to you to learn; this material may be old hat to you, but it's new to them. So speak clearly, maintain a steady pace, and stay calm.

Navigating Through a Slide Show

You can use the mouse and/or simple keyboard commands to move through a slide show. These are the easiest ways to navigate from one slide to the next.

The Slide Show Toolbar

The Slide Show toolbar is your navigator during the slide show. It is hidden when a slide show starts but becomes visible when you move your mouse around or point to the lower-left area of the screen. The Slide Show toolbar can be used to navigate a slide show or to draw attention to a specific area on a slide. However, use of this toolbar is unnecessary when you present a simple slide show like this one.

Navigate to the previous or next slide.

Draw with a pen, highlighter, or laser pointer, or erase a drawing.

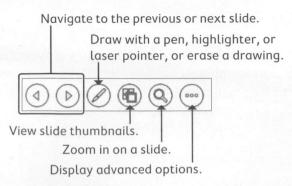

View slide thumbnails.

Zoom in on a slide.

Display advanced options.

 View the video "The Slide Show Toolbar."

≡ Advance one slide: [Spacebar], [→], [Page Down], *or* [Enter]

≡ Back up one slide: [Backspace], [←], *or* [Page Up]

DEVELOP YOUR SKILLS: P1-D8

In this exercise, you will navigate through your slide show.

1. Follow these steps to start the slide show:

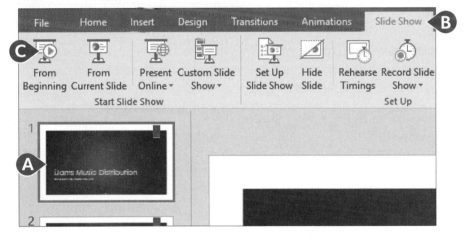

Ⓐ Click the title slide in the Slides panel to select it.

Ⓑ Click the **Slide Show** tab.

Ⓒ Choose **Start Slide Show→From Beginning**.

2. Move the mouse pointer around the screen for a moment.

Notice the Slide Show 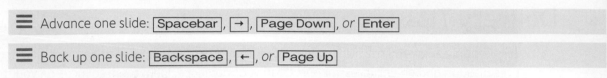 toolbar that appears near the bottom-left corner of the screen when the slides are in full-screen view.

3. Click the mouse pointer anywhere on the screen to move to the next slide.

4. Tap [Page Down] twice and then tap [Page Up] twice by using the keys near the main keyboard (not the keys on the numeric keypad).

PowerPoint displays the next or previous slide each time you tap these keys.

5. Follow these steps to use the Slide Show toolbar:

A Point to the lower-left area of the slide to display the Slide Show toolbar.

B Click **Show All Slides** to display thumbnails of all slides.

6. Click the **Packaging Options** slide.

As you can see, there are many ways to navigate slides in an electronic slide show.

End the Slide Show

7. Continue to click anywhere on the screen until the last slide appears (the Questions slide).

8. Click once on the last slide.

The screen turns to a black background, with a small note at the top.

9. Click anywhere on the black screen to exit the slide show and return to the main PowerPoint window.

Feel free to practice running your slide show again.

10. Choose **File→Close** to close the presentation and then exit PowerPoint.

Self-Assessment

 Check your knowledge of this chapter's key concepts and skills using the Self-Assessment in your ebook or eLab course.

⊥ Reinforce Your Skills

Create a Basic Presentation

In this exercise, you will begin to create a presentation for the Kids for Change organization—a community-based organization that helps socially aware youth plan and organize events that benefit their community. The presentation will be used to recruit new members and will be shown in high schools across the country.

1. Start PowerPoint and create a new blank presentation.
2. Save the presentation to your file storage location as **P1-R1-Kids**.
3. Choose **Design**→**Themes** and apply the **Facet** design theme.
4. Choose **Design**→**Variants** and apply the second variant (blue).
5. Click in the title placeholder and type **Kids for Change**.
6. Click in the subtitle placeholder and type **I can make a difference**.
7. Save the presentation and leave it open for the next exercise. *CTIL S*

Add Slides and Deliver a Presentation

In this exercise, you will complete the Kids for Change recruitment presentation by adding slides and text. Finally, you will deliver the presentation.

1. With the **P1-R1-Kids** presentation still open, choose **File**→**Save As** and save it as **P1-R2-Kids**.

Add Slides

2. Choose **Home**→**Slides**→**New Slide** 🖼.
3. Choose **Home**→**Slides**→**Layout menu button** ▼→**Two Content**.
4. Click in the title placeholder and type **Events**.
5. Add the following text to the bulleted list on the left:
   - iRecycling Day
   - Toy Collection
   - Shave and a Haircut
   - Diversity Festival
6. Add the following text to the bulleted list on the right:
   - Build-a-House
   - Bully No More
   - Adopt a Street
   - Tutoring

7. Save your presentation.

After completing a significant portion of work, it's a good idea to save what you've done before continuing.

8. Add a new slide with the title **Program Benefits** and notice it is already using the Two Content layout.

9. Add the following text and indentation to the bulleted list on the left:

▶ Personal

   ▶ **College application**   *Tab*

   ▶ **Leadership skills**

   ▶ **Sense of accomplishment**

10. Add the following text and indentation to the bulleted list on the right:

▶ Community

   ▶ **Crime reduction**

   ▶ **Increased literacy**

   ▶ **Improved health**

11. Add a new slide with the title **Requirements**.

12. Change the slide layout to **Title and Content**.

13. Type the following bullet points in the text box:
    - **You need**
    - **Positive attitude**
    - **Strong work ethic**
    - **Time commitment**
    - **One monthly event**
    - **One annual meeting**

14. Select the *Positive attitude* and *Strong work ethic* paragraphs and choose **Home→Paragraph→Increase List Level** .

15. Select the *One monthly event* and *One annual meeting* paragraphs and choose **Home→Paragraph→Increase List Level** .

16. Add a new slide with the title **Regional Contact** and notice that it is already using the Title and Content layout.

17. Type the following in the text box:
    - **Angelica Escobedo**
    - **(800) 555-0101**

18. Click the dashed border of the text box to select it.

19. Choose **Home→Paragraph→Bullets**  to remove the bullets from the text.

20. Choose **Home→Paragraph→Center** ▤ to center both paragraphs on the slide.

21. Save the presentation.

Deliver the Slide Show

22. Choose **Slide Show→Start Slide Show→From Beginning**.

The slide show starts from the first slide regardless of which slide is currently selected.

23. Navigate through the presentation by clicking the screen until the presentation is ended.

24. Click once more to return to the PowerPoint program window.

25. Choose **Slide Show→Start Slide Show→From Beginning** to start the slide show from the beginning again.

26. Move your mouse to the bottom-left corner of the screen to display the Slide Show toolbar.

27. Click the **Show All Slides** 🔳 button on the toolbar to display all the slide thumbnails.

28. Click the **Program Benefits** slide to go directly to it.

29. Tap [Esc] to end the slide show.

30. Exit PowerPoint.

REINFORCE YOUR SKILLS: P1-R3

Create an Events Promotion Presentation

In this exercise, you will create and deliver a new Kids for Change presentation to advertise upcoming events.

1. Start PowerPoint and create a new blank presentation.

2. Save the presentation to your file storage location as **P1-R3-Kids**.

3. Choose **Design→Themes** and apply the **Slice** theme.

4. Choose **Design→Variants** and apply the fourth theme variation (orange).

5. Add the title **Kids for Change** and the subtitle **June Event**.

6. Add a new slide with the title **Shave and a Haircut**.

7. Add the following bulleted text:

- **Free haircuts**
- **Free shaves**
- **Free mustache and beard trimming**

8. Save your presentation.

9. Add a new slide with the title **Participating Locations.**

10. Choose **Home→Slides→Layout menu button ▼→Two Content**.

11. Type the following, with indentations, in the left text box:

> ▶ Barbers
>> ▶ Sam the Barber
>> ▶ Hats Off
>> ▶ Clean Cuts

12. Type the following, with indentations, in the right text box:

> ▶ Shelters
>> ▶ Shelter on Main
>> ▶ Helping Hand
>> ▶ Safe Night

13. Add a new slide with the title **Dates and Availability.**

14. Choose **Home→Slides→Layout menu button ▼→Title and Content**.

15. Type the following bullet points in the text box:

- **All Locations**
- **Every Saturday in June**
- **8:00am – 8:00pm**
- **Availability**
- **Free service to help our community's homeless**

16. Select the two paragraphs under *All Locations* and increase their list level.

17. Select the last paragraph and increase its list level.

18. Add a final slide with the title **Sponsored By**.

19. Click the dashed border to select the entire Title text box.

20. Choose **Home→Paragraph→Center** to center the text on the slide.

21. Type **Kids for Change** in the text box.

22. Click the dashed border to select the entire text box.

23. Choose **Home→Paragraph→Bullets** to remove the bullets from the text.

24. Choose **Home→Paragraph→Center** to center the text on the slide.

25. Save your presentation.

Deliver the Slide Show

26. Choose **Slide Show→Start Slide Show→From Beginning**.

27. Click through the presentation until it has ended.

28. Return to the main PowerPoint window.

29. Start the slide show from the beginning again.

30. Click the **Show All Slides** button on the toolbar to display all the slide thumbnails and navigate directly to the **Participating Locations** slide.

31. Tap [Esc] to end the slide show and then exit PowerPoint.

✎ Apply Your Skills

APPLY YOUR SKILLS: P1-A1

Begin a Presentation

In this exercise, you will begin to create a new promotional presentation for Universal Corporate Events, a meeting and event planning service that handles event planning for businesses.

1. Start PowerPoint and then create a new blank presentation named **P1-A1-Events** in your file storage location.
2. Apply the **Ion** design theme.
3. Apply the fourth variation (reddish orange).
4. Add the following text to the title slide:
   - Title: `Universal Corporate Events`
   - Subtitle: `Events made easy`
5. Save your presentation.

APPLY YOUR SKILLS: P1-A2

Add Slides and Deliver a Presentation

In this exercise, you will complete the Universal Corporate Events presentation and deliver a slide show.

1. With the **P1-A1-Events** presentation from the previous exercise still open, save it as **P1-A2-Events**.
2. Add a second slide with the following text:

Title	`Event Types`
Bulleted paragraphs	`Celebrations`
	`Team building`
	`Tradeshows`
	`Ceremonies`

3. Add a third slide with the following text:

Title	`Services`
Bulleted paragraphs	`Venue scouting`
	`Catering`
	`Invitations`
	`Stage and sound equipment`

4. Add a fourth slide, change its layout to **Two Content**, and add the following text:

Title	Benefits
Left bulleted paragraphs	Our jobs
	Deal with paperwork
	Guarantee safety
	Scheduling
Right bulleted paragraphs	Your jobs
	Relax
	Enjoy your event

5. Select all but the first bullet in the left text box and increase the list level.

6. Select all but the first bullet in the right text box and increase the list level.

7. Add a final slide to the presentation and apply the **Section Header** layout.
   - Title: **Universal Corporate Events**
   - Text: **Events made easy**

8. Center both the title and the paragraph on the slide.

9. Save the presentation.

Deliver the Slide Show

10. Start the slide show from the beginning.

11. Advance to the second slide.

12. Use the Slide Show toolbar to display all the slides and then jump to the **Benefits** slide.

13. Continue navigating the slides until the slide show ends and you are returned to the main PowerPoint window.

14. Exit PowerPoint.

APPLY YOUR SKILLS: P1-A3

Create a Services Presentation

In this exercise, you will create a new presentation for Universal Corporate Events that outlines each of its services.

1. Start PowerPoint, create a new blank presentation, and save it to your file storage location as **P1-A3-Events**.

2. Apply the **Retrospect** theme.

3. Apply the third variation.

4. Add the title **Universal Corporate Events**.

5. Add the subtitle **Services**.

6. Add a second slide with the following text:

Title	Venue Scouting
Bulleted paragraphs	Locate three potential venues
	Provide digital tour
	Provide transportation for up to four

7. Add a third slide with the following text:

Title	Catering
Bulleted paragraphs	Vegetarian and vegan options
	Kosher options
	Never frozen

8. Add a fourth slide, change its layout to **Two Content**, and add the following text:

Title	Invitations
Left bulleted paragraphs	Creative
	Graphic design
	Matching envelopes
Right bulleted paragraphs	Business
	Create mailing labels
	Mail first class

9. Select all but the first bullet in the left text box and increase the list level.

10. Select all but the first bullet in the right text box and increase the list level.

11. Add a fifth slide to the presentation, apply the **Title and Content** layout, and add the following text:

Title	Stage and Sound Equipment
Bulleted paragraphs	Speaker podium and PA
	1,200-watt sound system for bands
	Portable dance floor

12. Add a final slide to the presentation and apply the **Section Header** layout.

13. Add the title **Thank you!** and the text **Hope to see you soon**.

14. Center both the title and text on the slide.

15. Save the presentation.

Deliver the Slide Show

16. Start the slide show from the beginning.

17. Advance to the second slide.

18. Use the **Slide Show** toolbar to display all the slides and then jump to the **Catering** slide.

19. Continue navigating the slides until the slide show ends and you are returned to the main PowerPoint window.

20. Exit PowerPoint.

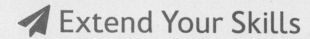

Extend Your Skills

These exercises challenge you to think critically and apply your new skills. You will be evaluated on your ability to follow directions, completeness, creativity, and the use of proper grammar and mechanics. Save files to your chapter folder. Submit assignments as directed.

P1-E1   That's the Way I See It

In this exercise, you will create a presentation for a charity that you feel strongly about in order to educate others about it. First, decide on a known charity you support or agree with. If you don't know of any charities, think of a few ideas for charities (such as saving animals or the environment, ensuring human rights, curing disease, etc.). Then use the Internet to find a reputable charity that deals with one of those topics.

Create a new, blank presentation named **P1-E1-Charity**. Apply the design theme and variation of your choice. Type the charity name as the slide title and type a short, descriptive phrase for the subtitle. Add a Title and Content slide that lists at least four actions the charity takes toward bettering its cause. Add a Two Content slide. On the left, list a few facts about the charity. On the right, list ways to donate to the charity. Create a final slide with the Section Header layout that duplicates the content shown on the title slide. View the presentation as a slide show and make a mental note of anything you want to change. When the slide show ends, make your changes and then save your presentation.

P1-E2   Be Your Own Boss

Your landscaping business, Blue Jean Landscaping, saves its customers money by having them share in the physical labor. In this exercise, you will create multiple slides with varying layouts and bulleted text to advertise your unique business to potential investors.

To begin, create a new, blank presentation named **P1-E2-BlueJean**. Apply the desired design theme and variation. Use the company name as the slide title and create a catchy phrase for the subtitle. Add a Title and Content slide that lists four services your company provides. Add a Two Content slide that lists the mutual benefits to the company and the customer: the left column uses *Us* as the first bullet, and the right column uses *You* as the first bullet. Then list at least three benefits for the company (left) and at least three for the customer (right). Increase the list level of all bullets except the first in each column.

Create a final slide with the Section Header layout that duplicates the content on the title slide. Run the slide show. Use the Slide Show toolbar to navigate the slide show and experiment with the other buttons on the toolbar.

P1-E3   Demonstrate Proficiency

Stormy BBQ, a restaurant featuring fresh, locally grown vegetables and local, farm-raised pork/beef, is considering expanding to new locations. Create a new presentation, named **P1-E3-Stormy**, to show at a local town hall meeting to convince the local residents and community leaders that Stormy BBQ would be a great fit for their community.

Use an appropriate theme for the business and its commitment to the community. Perhaps search for additional themes from the PowerPoint Start screen. Create at least five slides, including the title slide, with a different layout for each slide. At least one slide should include bullet points with varying list levels.

2

Designing and Printing the Presentation

I n this chapter, you will build on the fundamental design of the iJams presentation. To add professional credibility and make your presentation easier for an audience to follow, you will establish a consistent style throughout the presentation and format and organize the text. To make the presentation easier for you to create and manage, you will use a Microsoft Word outline to help auto-create slides that you will organize into sections. Finally, you will examine printing options, allowing you to provide your audience with take-home material.

LEARNING OBJECTIVES

▸ Use Outline view to create, move, and delete slides and edit text

▸ Create a presentation from a Microsoft Word outline

▸ Format and align text and adjust character spacing and line spacing

▸ Use Slide Sorter view and Sections

▸ Print a presentation

Project: Designing a Presentation

Now that the initial slides of the iJams presentation are complete, you need to make sure that the style is consistent throughout the presentation. A consistent style appears more organized, is easier for an audience to follow, and adds professional credibility. You must also ensure that the slides are in a logical sequence so the presentation is clear.

Working with Slides

As your presentation progresses and you insert additional slides, you may want to change the slide layout or order. For example, some slides may require two columns of bulleted text while others require only one. PowerPoint makes it easy to change the slide order by using Slide Sorter view.

Copying Text and Objects

You can move and copy text and objects by using drag and drop or the Cut, Copy, and Paste commands. It is usually most efficient to use drag and drop if you are moving or copying text or objects within a slide. Drag and drop is also effective for rearranging slides. Cut, Copy, and Paste are most efficient when moving or copying to a location not visible on the current screen.

DEVELOP YOUR SKILLS: P2-D1

In this exercise, you will add a new slide to a presentation, enter a bulleted list, and change the slide layout. You can always change a slide's layout after it has been created.

1. Start PowerPoint, open **P2-D1-Design** from the **PowerPoint Chapter 2** folder, and save it as **P2-D1-DesignRevised**.

   It's a good idea to append Revised *or something similar when editing and saving an existing presentation (or any document), as it leaves the original untouched in case you need to go back and start over.*

2. Select the **Our Services** slide from the Slides panel on the left side of your screen.

   The Our Services slide appears. New slides are inserted after the selected slide.

3. Choose **Home→Slides→New Slide** ▣.

4. Click in the title placeholder and type **Products and Promotional Items**.

5. Click in the bulleted list placeholder and type this list:
   - **Audio CDs**
   - **Downloadable MP3s**
   - **T-shirts**
   - **Baseball caps**
   - **Stickers**

- Pencils
- Key chains
- Posters
- Mugs
- Mouse pads

When you begin typing Mugs, PowerPoint reformats the bullets with a smaller font size so they all fit in the box. As you type the last bullet point, the font gets even smaller. A long list of bullets can be overwhelming, so strive for no more than six bullets. If there is more information, consider breaking the list into two columns. You will use this technique next by choosing a different layout for the slide.

6. Choose **Home→Slides→Layout menu button ▼→Two Content**.

   PowerPoint applies the Two Content layout to the current slide.

7. Follow these steps to move the last five bullets to the second box:

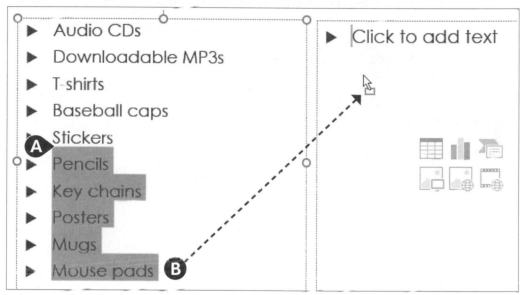

Ⓐ Select the last five bulleted paragraphs.

Ⓑ Drag the selected paragraphs to the right column.

This action moves the last five bulleted paragraphs into the right-side content area.

8. Save the changes to your presentation.

Working with Outlines

Although you have been working primarily in the slide to add or format text, the Outline panel is an alternative way to add, remove, and move text. The Outline panel is a useful interface to organize and structure your presentation.

The Outline Panel

The Outline panel helps you edit and reorganize slides. It's available on the left side of the screen in Outline view. You can type directly in the Outline panel to add or edit text on a slide. You can also select text from the Outline panel and format it with the standard Ribbon formatting commands. Any changes made in the Outline panel are immediately reflected in the actual slide.

 View the video "Using the Outline Panel."

☰ Add a new slide: Place the mouse pointer in the last group of bulleted paragraphs on a slide and press Ctrl + Enter

---

DEVELOP YOUR SKILLS: P2-D2

In this exercise, you will work with the Outline panel to add text.

1. Save your file as **P2-D2-DesignRevised**.
2. Choose **View→Presentation Views→Outline View**.
3. In the Outline panel, click anywhere in the **Our Services** slide title to select it.

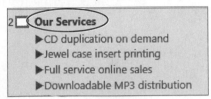

4. Press Ctrl + Enter.

   The insertion point moves to the first bulleted paragraph in the slide.

5. Press Ctrl + Enter again.

   PowerPoint creates a new slide below the selected slide.

6. Follow these steps to add text to the new slide while in the Outline panel:

   Ⓐ Type **Current Artists** here. Notice that the text also appears in the main portion of your window.

   Ⓑ Press Ctrl + Enter to move to the first bulleted paragraph.

   Ⓒ Type these bulleted paragraphs, tapping Enter (*not* Ctrl + Enter) after each, including the last bulleted line. You should see a blank fourth bullet in the Outline panel.

   PowerPoint adds a new slide to the presentation whenever the insertion point is positioned within the last paragraph on a slide and the Ctrl + Enter keystroke combination is issued. At this point, you should have a new, bulleted paragraph visible in the outline below the Da Grind paragraph.

7. Ensure that the insertion point is on the blank bulleted paragraph in the outline.

8. Choose **Home→Paragraph→Decrease List Level** ⊟.

   PowerPoint promotes the bulleted paragraph to create a new slide.

9. Type **New Artist Specials** and tap Enter.

   Tapping Enter created a new slide. You must use Ctrl + Enter to add a bulleted paragraph after a slide's title. However, you will fix this by demoting the new slide in the next step.

10. Choose **Home→Paragraph→Increase List Level** ⊟.

    The new slide created when you tapped Enter in step 9 has been converted to a bullet under the New Artist Specials title.

11. Complete the new slide in the outline as shown, tapping Enter after each paragraph (including the last one):
    - **25% discount on CD duplication** Enter
    - **Five free T-shirts** Enter
    - **10% discount on promotional items** Enter
    - **Valid until July 20** Enter

12. Choose **Home→Paragraph→Decrease List Level** ⊟ to promote the new paragraph that follows the *Valid until July 20* paragraph and convert it into a new slide.

13. Type **Contact Us** and then press Ctrl + Enter to create a bullet below the title.

14. Taking care not to tap Enter after the last bullet in this slide, complete the new slide as shown:
    - **Call** Enter
    - **(800) 555-0101** Enter
    - **Or** Enter
    - **Email us at** Enter
    - **iJams@example.com**

15. Save your presentation.

Collapsing and Expanding Slides

As the Outline panel grows, it can be difficult to manage your slides when all the bulleted text is showing. PowerPoint lets you collapse slides so that only the title is visible. This makes it easier to manage your slides because more slides will be visible in the Outline panel.

DEVELOP YOUR SKILLS: P2-D3

In this exercise, you will use the context menu from the Outline panel to collapse, expand, and move sides.

1. Save your file as **P2-D3-DesignRevised**.

2. Follow these steps to explore the Outline panel:

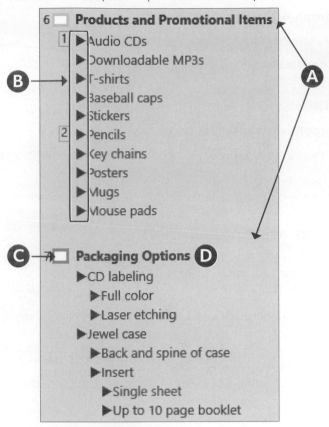

Ⓐ Scroll until *Products and Promotional Items* and *Packaging Options* are visible.

Each slide is represented by an icon. Slides with multiple bulleted lists use numbers for identification.

Ⓑ Click any **bullet** icon in the Products and Promotional Items slide to select the bulleted text.

Ⓒ Click this **slide** icon to select all text on the slide.

Ⓓ Click to the right of the **Packaging Options** title text (outside the highlighted area) to deselect the slide.

3. Double-click the **Products and Promotional Items slide** icon.

The bulleted paragraphs beneath the title are collapsed and hidden.

4. Double-click the **Products and Promotional Items slide** icon again.

The bulleted paragraphs beneath the title are expanded and are once again visible.

5. Right-click anywhere in the **Outline** panel and choose **Collapse→Collapse All**.

All bulleted paragraphs are collapsed and hidden. Only the slide titles remain visible.

6. Right-click anywhere (except on text) in the **Outline** panel and choose **Expand→Expand All**.

All bulleted paragraphs are expanded and are once again visible.

Move a Slide

The easiest way to move a slide in an outline is to first collapse all slides. Then you can click the desired slide title and drag it to its new position.

7. Right-click anywhere in the **Outline** panel and choose **Collapse→Collapse All**.

8. If necessary, scroll up until all slide icons and titles are visible in the **Outline** panel.

9. Follow these steps to move a slide:

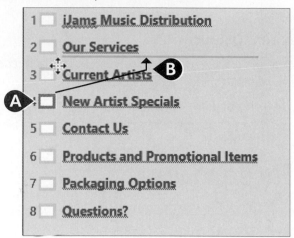

Ⓐ Click the **New Artist Specials slide** icon to select the entire slide.

Ⓑ Drag the **slide** icon up until a line appears above the Current Artists slide and then release the mouse button.

The New Artist Specials slide appears above the Current Artists slide.

10. Using this same method, move the **Packaging Options** slide to the second position, just below the title slide. Your slides should be arranged in the following order.

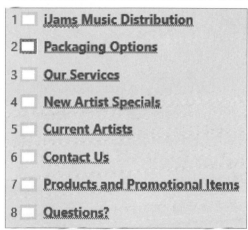

11. Save your presentation.

Deleting Slides

You can delete a slide from a presentation using the Outline panel, or in Normal or Slide Sorter views. If you inadvertently delete a slide, you can use the Undo button on the Quick Access toolbar to undo the latest action and restore the deleted slide. If you later decide that you want to keep the change, just use the Redo button!

DEVELOP YOUR SKILLS: P2-D4

In this exercise, you will delete slides using the Outline panel.

1. Save your file as **P2-D4-DesignRevised**.

2. Right-click anywhere in the **Outline** panel and choose **Expand→Expand All**.

3. Click the **Current Artists slide** icon (not the title text) to select the entire slide.

4. Tap ⟨Delete⟩ to remove the slide.

5. Using this same method, delete the **Questions** slide.

   A faded bullet may appear at the end of the previous slide. This is PowerPoint readying itself for additional text. The ghost bullet will not display on the slide itself.

6. Save your presentation and then choose **File→Close** to close it.

Working with Word Integration

Microsoft Word is an excellent word-processing program that integrates with PowerPoint. An outline created in Word can easily be converted to a PowerPoint presentation. You may need to create a presentation based on an outline someone else created in Word, or you may find it easier to plan a presentation using a Word outline rather than starting PowerPoint first and wondering what slides you will create.

Creating a Presentation Outline in Word

Word's powerful outlining tool makes setting up and modifying outlines easy. You can create an outline in Word and import it to PowerPoint. To use Word outlines in PowerPoint, you must apply the appropriate styles to the paragraphs in the Word document before importing the outline. PowerPoint converts the Word outline by using these rules:

▶ All level-1 paragraphs translate to titles in a PowerPoint slide.

▶ All level-2 paragraphs translate to level-1 body bullets in a PowerPoint slide.

▶ All level-3 paragraphs translate to level-2 body bullets in a PowerPoint slide.

After a Word outline has been imported into PowerPoint, you can promote or demote the bullets, apply layouts and a design theme, and make other enhancements.

This Word outline...   ...creates these PowerPoint slides.

DEVELOP YOUR SKILLS: P2-D5

In this exercise, you will create an outline in Word, use it to generate slides for a new presentation, and then modify the presentation.

1. Start Word and create a new, blank document named **P2-D5-WordOutline** saved to your file storage location.

   In the next few steps, you will type and apply Word styles to paragraphs.

2. With the blank document open, choose **View→Views→Outline**.

3. Type **iJams Music Distribution** and tap ⬚Enter⬚.

4. Tap ⬚Tab⬚, type **A Year of Success**, and tap ⬚Enter⬚.

   Tapping ⬚Tab⬚ increases the list level and creates a level-2 style.

5. Press ⬚Shift⬚+⬚Tab⬚, type **Online Downloads**, and tap ⬚Enter⬚.

   Pressing ⬚Shift⬚+⬚Tab⬚ decreases the list level and returns the text to a level-1 style.

   Next, you will create two level-2-styled paragraphs that will eventually be converted to text bullets in a PowerPoint slide.

6. Tap ⬚Tab⬚, type **MP3 sales exceed $1M**, and tap ⬚Enter⬚.

7. Type **350,000 new user accounts** and tap ⬚Enter⬚.

8. Press ⬚Shift⬚+⬚Tab⬚ to return the indentation level to a level-1 style.

   You are now ready to continue typing the rest of the outline.

9. Complete the rest of the outline as shown, using ⬚Enter⬚ to create new paragraphs and ⬚Tab⬚ and ⬚Shift⬚+⬚Tab⬚ to adjust indent levels.

   ⊕ iJams Music Distribution
   　　⊖ A Year of Success
   ⊕ Online Downloads
   　　⊖ MP3 sales exceed $1M
   　　⊖ 350,000 new user accounts
   ⊕ Promotional Items
   　　⊖ T-shirt sales exceed $500k
   　　⊖ Total promotional item sales exceed $1.5M
   ⊕ New Hires
   　　⊖ Jamal Lawrence – Webmaster
   　　⊖ Malika Fayza – Search Engine Specialist
   　　⊖ Jin Chen – Marketing Analyst
   ⊕ Thank You!
   　　⊖ Our Success Is Your Success

10. Save the file and then close the outline and Word.

    Word closes, and PowerPoint becomes visible.

Import the Outline

11. If necessary, restore PowerPoint from the taskbar (or start it).

12. Choose **File→New**, click the **Blank Presentation** icon, and save your file as `P2-D5-Word Outline` to your file storage location.

You can use the same filename as the Word document because the Word and PowerPoint files have different file extensions.

13. Choose **Design→Themes→More** ⊟→**Ion** to apply a document theme.

14. Locate the **Design→Variants** group on the Ribbon and click the third variation (the purple one) to apply it to all slides.

15. Choose **Home→Slides→New Slide menu button** ▼→**Slides from Outline**.

16. Use the Insert Outline dialog box to navigate to your file storage location.

17. Choose **P2-D5-WordOutline** and click **Insert**.

PowerPoint will take a moment to import the outline. Note that the first slide is blank because PowerPoint inserted the slides from the outline after the existing blank title slide.

18. Choose **View→Presentation Views→Outline View** and examine the PowerPoint outline.

Each level-1 paragraph from the outline has become a slide title, and each level-2 paragraph has become a bulleted paragraph under the appropriate title.

19. Choose **View→Presentation Views→Normal** to view the slide thumbnails.

20. Choose the first slide (the blank one) and tap Delete .

The blank slide is deleted, and the iJams Music Distribution slide becomes selected.

Change a Layout

21. Choose **Home→Slides→Layout** ▼→**Title Slide**.

The layout of the selected slide changes.

22. Select the final slide, **Thank You**, and choose **Home→Slides→Layout** ▼→**Section Header**.

23. Choose the first slide, **iJams Music Distribution**.

Each slide is formatted with blue text because Word formatted the heading styles as blue.

Reset the Slide Formatting

24. With the first slide selected, choose **Home→Slides→Reset**.

The text formatting is removed and returns to the default setting for the current document theme. The slide subtitle is converted to uppercase because that is the Ion theme's formatting.

25. Select the second slide, press Shift , select the last slide, and release Shift .

Slides 2–5 become selected.

26. Choose **Home→Slides→Reset** to reformat the text on the selected slides with the document theme formatting.

27. Save your presentation.

Formatting Your Presentation

PowerPoint makes it so easy to create a presentation that the slides you create may not need any additional formatting. After all, the placeholders arrange the text, the bullets are automatic, and the color scheme is preformatted. However, in most cases, you will want to fine-tune your presentation. Formatting your presentation will make it even better.

Formatting Text

Formatting text is a common step in presentation development. Using the Format Painter is great if something on the slide is already formatted as you want and you simply want to copy the formatting. However, sometimes you need to format text from scratch. For instance, when reviewing a slide, you might decide that the text could be emphasized by changing the font color. If you had the time, you could change the font color of each piece of text on the slide individually by using the Font group on the Ribbon's Home tab. However, a more efficient way to change the font color is to first select the placeholder and then apply the color change. By selecting the placeholder, all text within the placeholder is changed in one swoop.

 View the video "Formatting Text."

Character Spacing

Character spacing refers to the horizontal space between characters. PowerPoint lets you adjust this spacing to give your text some breathing room. If none of the preset options fit your needs, you can enter a numerical value to specify the exact amount of spacing. In the professional world of print, this is referred to as tracking or kerning. You must first select characters before applying character spacing, or select the placeholder to apply spacing to all the text.

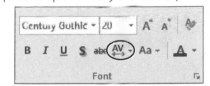

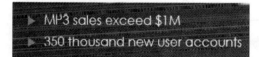 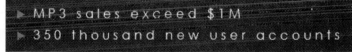

The same slide with no character spacing (left) and a large amount of character spacing applied (right)

Setting the Text Case

A quick way to populate your slides with text is to copy text from an existing source, such as from an email message or a Word document. However, the original text may not be formatted in the case appropriate for your slide. You can easily change the case of text, saving you from having to retype it.

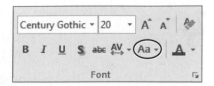

TEXT CASE OPTIONS

Menu Option	How It Affects Text
Sentence Case	Your text will look like this.
Uppercase	YOUR TEXT WILL LOOK LIKE THIS.
Capitalize Each Word	Your Text Will Look Like This.
Toggle Case	Wherever you typed an uppercase letter, it will become lowercase. Wherever you typed a lowercase letter, it will become uppercase. Example: If you type **Your Text Will Look Like This**, Toggle Case will change it to **yOUR tEXT wILL lOOK lIKE tHIS**.

DEVELOP YOUR SKILLS: P2-D6

In this exercise, you will change the font formatting in the title and subtitle.

1. Save your file as **P2-D6-WordOutline**.
2. Choose **View→Presentation Views→Normal** to return to Normal view, if necessary.
3. Display the **Home** tab so you can see the font settings as you work.
4. Click the title slide (the first one) in the Slides panel to select it.
5. Follow these steps to select the subtitle placeholder box:

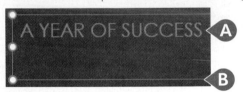

   Ⓐ Click anywhere on the subtitle text to position the insertion point inside the handles for this text box. The dashed line indicates the text box border.

   Ⓑ Click any edge of the dashed border to change it to a solid border (shown here).

   The solid line indicates that the text box is selected. Any formatting change you make now will affect all text within the box. Notice also that the Font Size box on the Ribbon is currently set to 20. The Ion theme applied this font size to the subtitle.

6. Choose **Home→Font→Increase Font Size** Â to increase the font size to **24**.
7. Choose **Home→Font→Bold** B .
8. Choose **Home→Font→Shadow** S .

   The text stands out from the page a bit more because there is now a slight drop-shadow effect.

Format the Title

9. Click on the title text, *iJams Music Distribution*, and then click once on the dashed-line border to select the **Title** text box.
10. Choose **Home→Font→Font Size menu button** ▼ and point to several different font sizes.

    Notice how Live Preview displays the slide title size changes as you point to different settings on the Font Size menu.

11. Set the font size to **96**.

The text is not large enough. There is still some room to enlarge it so that the company name dominates the slide.

12. Click **96** in the **Home→Font→Font Size menu button ▼**.

13. Type **115** and tap ⟦Enter⟧.

PowerPoint increases the text size to 115. You can select a font size from the menu or type in your own value.

14. Save the presentation.

Setting Line Spacing

Sometimes, instead of changing the font size or adding many hard returns, you need to increase or decrease only the spacing between lines to have the proper effect. Line spacing determines the amount of space between lines of text. This setting is useful if text appears cramped and you wish to open up some breathing room between lines.

The same slide before and after applying line spacing

DEVELOP YOUR SKILLS: P2-D7

In this exercise, you will adjust the line spacing to increase the amount of space between bullets.

1. Save your file as **P2-D7-WordOutline**.

2. Display the **New Hires** slide.

3. Click any of the names to display a dashed border.

4. Click the dashed border to select the entire text box.

5. Choose **Home→Paragraph→Line Spacing** ▦ **menu button ▼→2.0** to increase the spacing.

PowerPoint redistributes the bulleted text vertically on the slide with more spacing between items.

6. Save and close your presentation.

Setting Paragraph Alignment

In time, you will be able to eye a presentation and notice if the paragraph alignment is not balanced. You can select one or more paragraphs and then click an alignment button on the Ribbon to make the change.

PARAGRAPH ALIGNMENT BUTTONS

Purpose	Button	Example
Left-align	≡	This text has been left-aligned. Notice how the left edge is in a straight line, but the right edge appears jagged. This is most noticeable with multiple lines of text.
Center	≡	This text has been center-aligned. Notice how the text on both lines is balanced and centered.
Right-align	≡	This text has been right-aligned. Notice how the right edge is in a straight line.
Justify	≡	This text has been justified. Notice how the text is spaced to maintain straight lines on the left and right. This is most noticeable when there are multiple lines of text.

 Tip! *It is often easiest to read left-aligned text because the eye can more easily find the starting point of subsequent lines.*

≡ Home→Paragraph→Align Left ≡, Center ≡, Align Right ≡, *or* Justify ≡

DEVELOP YOUR SKILLS: P2-D8

In this exercise, you will reformat a slide.

1. Open **P2-D8-Contact** from your **PowerPoint Chapter 2** folder and save it as **P2-D8-ContactRevised**.

2. If necessary, scroll down; select the **Contact Us** slide (slide 5).

3. Click in the bulleted list and then click a border of the text box.

4. Choose **Home→Paragraph→Bullets** ⫴ to remove the bullets.

5. Choose **Home→Paragraph→Center** ≡.

6. Select the entire telephone number.

   A formatting box appears. You may format the selected text from this formatting box, but we will use the Ribbon as in the next steps.

7. Choose **Home→Font→Font Size menu button** ▼ and increase the size to **32**.

8. Click anywhere inside the phone number and then choose **Home→Clipboard→Format Painter** 🖌 to copy the formatting.

9. Click anywhere inside the email address to paste the formatting so that its font size is increased to 32.

10. Save your presentation.

Using the Slide Sorter

Up until now, you've been working in Normal view, which is good for manipulating a handful of slides. However, as your presentation grows to more slides than are visible in Normal view, you will want to explore the function of Slide Sorter view.

PowerPoint's Slide Sorter view is used to rearrange slides. In Slide Sorter view, each slide is a thumbnail image so the entire presentation is visible at a glance. As your presentation grows, often the slide order needs to be changed to create a logical concept flow. Using the drag-and-drop method in Slide Sorter view is a great way to quickly reorganize slides.

DEVELOP YOUR SKILLS: P2-D9

In this exercise, you will use Slide Sorter view to rearrange the slide order.

1. Save your file as **P2-D9-ContactRevised**.
2. Choose **View→Presentation Views→Slide Sorter** ⊞.
3. Follow these steps to move a slide:

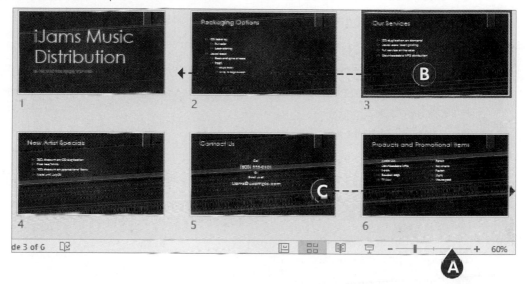

- **A** If necessary, drag the **Zoom** slider to change the zoom percentage until all six slides are shown. (Your slides may display differently.)
- **B** Drag the **Our Services** slide to the left of Packaging Options to make it the second slide.
- **C** Drag the **Contact Us** slide to the end of the presentation.
4. Choose **View→Presentation Views→Normal** ⊞.
5. Save and close the presentation.

Organizing with Sections

Using the Slide Sorter with individual slides works well for small presentations. For presentations containing many slides, PowerPoint's Section feature helps you keep them organized.

Sections are always created before the selected slide and include all following slides. This often results in a section containing more slides than intended. The fix is to simply create another section after the intended last slide.

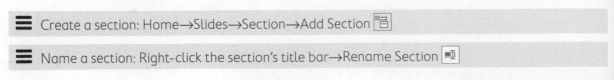

≡ Create a section: Home→Slides→Section→Add Section

≡ Name a section: Right-click the section's title bar→Rename Section

DEVELOP YOUR SKILLS: P2-D10

In this exercise, you will create sections.

1. Open **P2-D10-Sections** from your **PowerPoint Chapter 2** folder and save it as **P2-D10-SectionsRevised**.

   With so many slides, it may be easier to work in Slide Sorter view.

2. Choose **View→Presentation Views→Slide Sorter**.

3. Select **Artist Successes** (slide 2) and then choose **Home→Slides→Section ▼→Add Section**.

   A new section named Untitled Section *is created before the selected slide. Every slide below it is included in the section.*

4. Follow these steps to rename the section:

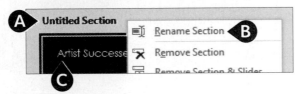

   Ⓐ Right-click the *Untitled Section* title bar.

   Ⓑ Choose **Rename Section**.

   Ⓒ Type **Artist success** and click the **Rename** button.

   The section is renamed but contains slides not intended for this section.

5. Select **Our Services** (slide 6) and then choose **Home→Slides→Section ▼→Add Section**.

   A new section is started before the selected slide. PowerPoint may scroll the Slide Sorter window to the top of the presentation depending on your screen resolution.

6. Scroll down until you see the new, untitled section.

7. Right-click the *Untitled Section* title bar, choose **Rename Section**, and rename the section to **Products and services**.

8. Click the last slide, **Contact Us**, and create a new section before it.

9. Rename the final section `Call to action`.

10. Save your presentation.

Managing Sections

After sections have been created, they can be dragged and rearranged in either the Slides panel or Slide Sorter view. Individual slides can even be dragged from one section to another. Additionally, sections can be collapsed, similar to slide titles in Outline view. Collapsed sections hide the slides, making it easy to drag and reorder the sections. However, the collapsed sections hide slides only when editing. The collapsed slides will display as normal when running the slide show.

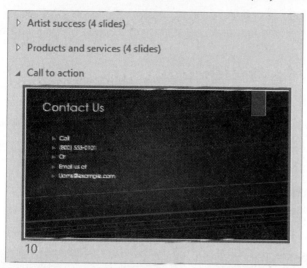

Collapsing sections reduces clutter in the Slides panel. When collapsed, the section title bar indicates how many slides exist in that section.

≣ Collapse or expand a section: Double-click a section's title bar

≣ Remove a section: Right-click the section's title bar→choose desired Remove option

DEVELOP YOUR SKILLS: P2-D11

In this exercise, you will rearrange slides by using sections.

1. Save your presentation as **P2-D11-SectionsRevised**.

2. With the presentation still displaying Slide Sorter view, scroll until you can see the *Artist success* section title bar, if necessary.

3. Double-click the **Artist success** section title bar to collapse it.

4. Double-click the **Products and services** section title bar to collapse it, too.

5. Choose **View→Presentation Views→Normal**.

   The sections do not remain collapsed when you change views.

6. Follow these steps to rearrange the sections:

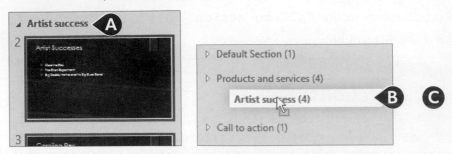

Ⓐ Scroll until you see the *Artist success* section title bar.

Ⓑ Drag the **Artist success** title below the *Products and services* section. As you start to drag, the sections collapse.

Ⓒ Release the mouse button when the *Artist success* section is placed properly. The sections expand again.

7. Choose **View→Presentation Views→Slide Sorter**.

8. Click anywhere in the gray area outside the slide thumbnails to deselect any slides.

9. Scroll down, if necessary, until you see the entire *Call to action* section with the Contact Us slide.

10. Use the **Zoom** slider, if necessary, to make the view smaller so that you see all slides in both the *Products and services* and *Call to action* sections.

11. Drag the last slide of the *Products and services* section (**New Artist Specials**) to the left of the Contact Us slide to move it to the *Call to action* section.

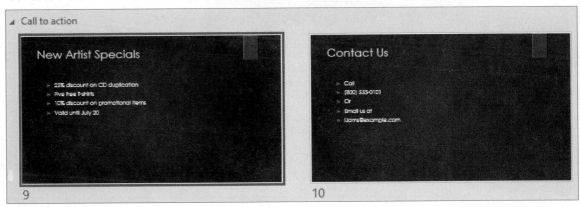

12. Save your presentation.

Printing Your Presentation

Most of the time, you will be viewing or projecting the presentations you create from a PC or laptop computer. However, there may be times when a hard copy of the presentation is needed.

PowerPoint can create the following types of printouts:

▸ **Slides:** Prints each slide of a presentation on a separate page

▸ **Handouts:** Prints one or more slides per page, leaving room for attendees to jot notes during the presentation

- **Speaker Notes:** Prints each slide on a separate page, with any speaker notes you created for the slide below

- **Outline:** Prints a text outline of each slide, similar to what is seen in the Outline panel

☰ File→Print │ [Ctrl]+[P]

The Print Shortcut

If you have customized your Quick Access toolbar to display the Quick Print icon, you may find it tempting to just click it. However, before this becomes a habit, know that a click of this button sends the entire presentation to the current printer, whether or not you want to make adjustments. If you are working with a document theme that has a colored background, the printing process will not only be painstakingly slow, but it may also waste your toner or ink!

The Quick Print button on the Quick Access toolbar sends your presentation directly to the printer.

Printing Handouts

You can reinforce your presentation's main points by providing handouts. Participants will be able to walk away from your presentation with more than a vague memory of your slide show; all of the facts you presented during the presentation will go with them as a reference. Handouts can be printed in a range of layouts, from two to nine slides per page. For example, printing three slides on a page places three small slides on the left side and multiple lines on the right for note taking.

☰ File→Print→Settings→Print Layout menu button ▼→select a handout layout

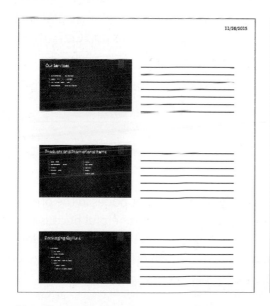

Handout with three slides per page

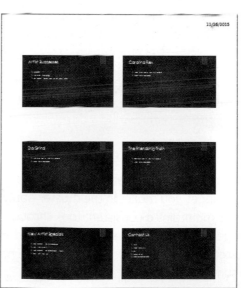

Handout with six slides per page

In this exercise, you will use Backstage view to preview a printout of basic handouts.

1. Choose **File→Print**.
2. Follow these steps to examine the print options:

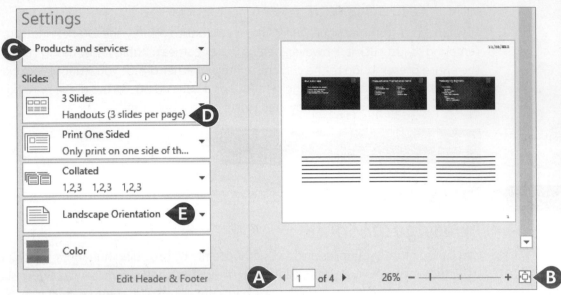

Ⓐ Use the left arrow to return to the first slide.

Ⓑ Click the **Zoom to Page** button so the whole slide fits in the preview. If your printer is not a color printer, your slide preview will display in black and white.

Ⓒ Choose **Sections→Products and services** to print the three slides in that section.

Ⓓ Choose **Handouts→3 Slides**. Changing this option to anything other than Full Page Slides causes the Orientation option to appear between the Collated and Color options.

Ⓔ Change this option to **Landscape Orientation**.

3. Click the **Back** button at the top of **Backstage** view to return to the main PowerPoint screen without printing.

Handout Masters

In any presentation, there is a single handout master that controls the format of the handout sheets. Any changes you make on the master apply instantly to all handout pages in the presentation. The master maintains a consistent look throughout your handout. This is helpful because you need to change only a single handout master, and the layout, look, and feel of multiple handouts will be affected. Options that you can set on the handout master, which affect all printed handout sheets, are summarized below.

 View the video "Handout Masters."

≡ View→Master Views→Handout Master

≡ Handout Master→Close→Close Master View ✕

Handout Headers and Footers

You can set up a header and footer to print on all pages of a handout. These work just like headers and footers in a word-processor document. Headers appear at the top, or head, of a document. Footers appear at the bottom, or foot, of a document. Headers and footers often include the presenter's name, occasion, date, and other information, which is helpful when attendees reference the handouts later, after the presentation.

Green Clean End of Year Review		Presented on 12/2/2015

These headers will print at the top of each handout page.

DEVELOP YOUR SKILLS: P2-D13

In this exercise, you will add the date and event to the header and footer of the handouts. The handouts will then be previewed in a special print layout.

1. Save the presentation as **P2-D13-SectionsRevised**.
2. Choose **View→Master Views→Handout Master**.
3. Follow these steps to set up header sheets:

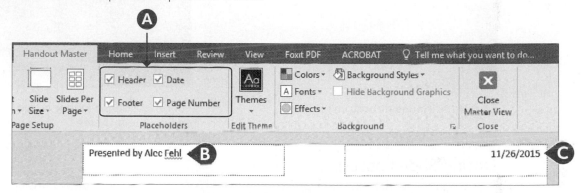

- Ⓐ Verify that all four of the Placeholders checkboxes have a checkmark.
- Ⓑ Scroll to the top of the handout, if necessary. Click in the **Header** area at the top-left corner of the document and type **Presented by [Your Name]**.
- Ⓒ Notice that the current date is automatically entered.

4. Scroll down to the bottom of the document, click in the bottom-left Footer placeholder, and type **iJams**.
5. Choose **Handout Master→Close→Close Master View** to return to the presentation.

Preview the Custom Handouts

6. Choose **File→Print**.

   Notice that your previous print settings were saved and that the preview shows the layout of the three slides with your new custom header.

7. Click the **Back** ⊖ button at the top of Backstage view to return to the main PowerPoint screen without printing.
8. Save your presentation.

Slide Footers

Just as you can place a header or footer on a handout, you can also place footers on the slides in your presentation. Slide footers often display the date, event name, slide number, or other text that you want visible throughout the presentation. Although the term "footer" implies being inserted along the bottom of a slide, this will change depending on the slide layout and document theme. For example, some slide footers display along the top of the title slide. The same is true for the other elements, such as the slide number and date. These elements will display in different locations on a slide depending on the slide layout and document theme. Additionally, you may opt to display footers on all slides in the presentation, all slides except the title slide, or selected slides only.

 Slide footers and handout footers are completely separate settings.

Footer positioned at bottom of slide

Footer position changes based on document theme

Dating Slide Footers

If you choose to include the date, you will need to decide whether you want it updated automatically so your presentation always displays the current date/time or whether you prefer to type in a static date/time that never changes unless you edit it manually. If you choose to update automatically, you may display the date in several formats, including numbers only, day or month spelled out, and the time.

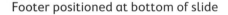

≡ Insert→Text→Header & Footer 📄

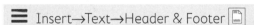

DEVELOP YOUR SKILLS: P2-D14

In this exercise, you will create a slide footer and apply it to all slides in the presentation.

1. Save the presentation as **P2-D14-SectionsRevised**.
2. Choose **View→Presentation Views→Normal**.
3. Choose the **Our Services** slide (slide 2).
4. Choose **Insert→Text→Header & Footer**.

5. Follow these steps to configure your footer:

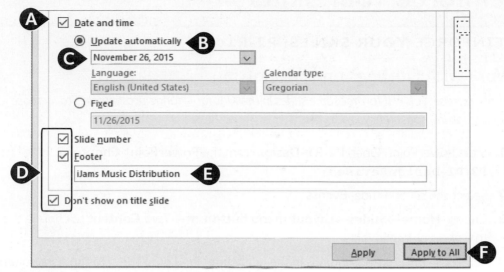

(A) Place a checkmark in the **Date and Time** checkbox.

(B) Choose the **Update Automatically** option.

(C) Choose the date format shown here from the menu.

(D) Place checkmarks in these three option boxes.

(E) Type **iJams Music Distribution** as the footer text.

(F) Click **Apply to All**.

PowerPoint applies the settings to all slides in the presentation. You could have chosen to apply the footer to just the currently displayed slide. The footer should appear on the right side of the slide, under the slide number, rotated 90 degrees. This is the current theme's design.

6. Browse through the presentation and notice that the footer appears on every slide except the title slide.

7. Save your presentation and close PowerPoint.

Printing Transparencies

In addition to printing handouts and slides to share with your audience, you can also print transparencies to use with an overhead projector, which displays printouts on a large screen similar to a movie projector. While there is no Print Transparency option in PowerPoint, you can simply print your slides, handouts, or notes onto transparency film if your printer supports it. You will need to check the documentation for your printer to learn how to specify transparency film, as the steps vary from printer to printer.

Self-Assessment

 Check your knowledge of this chapter's key concepts and skills using the Self-Assessment in your ebook or eLab course.

Reinforce Your Skills

Work with Outlines and Formatting

In this exercise, you will format some slides in the Kids for Change presentation to increase its visual appeal and formatting consistency.

1. Start PowerPoint. Open **P2-R1-Design** from the **PowerPoint Chapter 2** folder and save it as **P2-R1-DesignRevised**.

2. Select the second slide, **Events**.

3. Choose **Home→Slides→Layout menu button ▼→Two Content** to change the slide layout to a two-column layout.

4. Select the last four paragraphs in the left column and drag them to the right column.

Create Slides in the Outline Panel

5. Choose **View→Presentation Views→Outline View**.

6. Locate the Program Benefits slide in the Outline panel.

7. Click to the right of the word *health* in the last paragraph of the **Program Benefits** slide in the Outline panel.

8. Tap ⌈Ctrl⌉+⌈Enter⌉ to create a new slide.

Edit Slides in the Outline Panel

9. Type **Requirements** in the Outline panel as the slide title.

10. Tap ⌈Enter⌉ and then tap ⌈Tab⌉ to create a new bulleted paragraph.

11. Type **You need** in the Outline panel.

12. Tap ⌈Enter⌉ and then tap ⌈Tab⌉ to increase the list level of the new bulleted paragraph.

13. Type **Positive attitude**, tap ⌈Enter⌉, and type **Strong work ethic** to create another indented paragraph.

14. Tap ⌈Enter⌉ and then tap ⌈Shift⌉+⌈Tab⌉ to create and promote the next bullet.

15. Type **Time commitment**.

16. Tap ⌈Enter⌉ and then tap ⌈Tab⌉.

17. Type **One monthly event**, tap ⌈Enter⌉, and type **One annual meeting** to create the final two paragraphs.

18. Choose **Home→Slides→Layout menu button ▼→Title and Content**.

Format the Presentation

19. Choose **View→Presentation Views→Normal** and select the title slide from the **Slides** panel.

20. Click the **Title** box and then click again on the edge of the box to select it.

21. Choose **Home→Font→Increase Font Size** once to increase the font size to **60**.

22. Choose **Home→Font→Bold**.

23. Display the **Requirements** slide on the Slides panel.

24. Choose **Home→Slides→New Slide**.

25. Type **Remember** as the title.

26. Type the following as bulleted paragraphs:
    - **Think globally, act locally.**
    - **Or think locally, act globally.**
    - **Just...**
    - **Think and act!**

27. Select the bulleted text box by clicking the border.

28. Choose **Home→Paragraph→Bullets** to remove the bullets from all paragraphs.

29. Choose **Home→Paragraph→Center** to center the text on the slide.

30. Choose **Home→Paragraph→Line Spacing menu button ▼→2.0** to increase the vertical spacing between bullets.

31. Select the text *Think and act!*.

32. Choose **Home→Font→Increase Font Size** four times to increase the size to 32.

33. With the *Think and act!* text still selected, double-click the **Home→Clipboard→Format Painter** button to load it for multiple uses.

34. Click the words *Think and act* in the first line and then click the words *Think and act* in the second line to duplicate the formatting.

35. Choose **Home→Clipboard→Format Painter** to turn off the Format Painter.

36. Save the presentation and exit PowerPoint.

REINFORCE YOUR SKILLS: P2-R2

Create a Presentation Based on a Word Outline

In this exercise, you will import an outline from Word, create sections, rearrange sections and slides, and print a slide.

1. Start Word and open **P2-R2-Outline** from the **PowerPoint Chapter 2** folder.

2. Choose **View→Views→Outline**.

3. Read over the outline. Then close Word.

4. Start PowerPoint, click **Blank Presentation**, and save your file as **P2-R2-Outline** to your file storage location.

5. Choose **Design→Themes→Ion** to apply that design theme.

6. Choose **Home→Slides→New Slide menu button ▼→Slides from Outline** to begin importing the Word outline.

7. Navigate to your **PowerPoint Chapter 2** folder and double-click the **P2-R2-Outline** Word document to import the outline and create the slides.

8. Select slide 1 in the Slides panel and tap [Delete] to delete the blank slide.

9. Click slide 1 in the Slides panel to ensure it is selected, scroll to the bottom of the Slides panel, and [Shift]+click the final slide, slide 7, so all slides are selected.

10. Choose **Home→Slides→Reset** to reset the formatting of all slides.

11. Click slide 1 in the Slides panel to select it and deselect the others.

12. Choose **Home→Slides→Layout menu button ▼→Title Slide**.

Organize with Sections

13. Click the **College Application** slide (slide 2) in the Slides panel to select it and deselect the others.

14. Choose **Home→Slides→Section menu button ▼→Add Section** to add a new section starting with the College Application slide.

15. Choose **Home→Slides→Section menu button ▼→Rename Section**.

16. Type **Personal Benefits** and then click **Rename**.

17. Click the **Crime Reduction** slide (slide 4) in the Slides panel to select it and deselect the others.

18. Choose **Home→Slides→Section menu button ▼→Add Section** to add a new section starting with the Crime Reduction slide.

19. Choose **Home→Slides→Section menu button ▼→Rename Section**.

20. Type **Community Benefits** and then click **Rename**.

Organize with the Slide Sorter

21. Choose **View→Presentation Views→Slide Sorter**.

22. Drag the **Zoom** slider in the lower-right area of the PowerPoint window until all seven slides are visible.

23. Drag the **Leadership Skills** slide so it is between the College Application and Sense of Accomplishment slides.

24. Drag the **Community Benefits** section header up so that it is before the *Personal Benefits* section.

Add Slide and Handout Footers

25. Choose **View→Master Views→Handout Master**.

26. Click in the top-left placeholder and type **Presented by [Your Name]**.

27. Choose **Handout Master→Close→Close Master View**.

28. Choose **Insert→Text→Header & Footer**.

29. Check the box to display the date and time.

30. Check the box to include the slide number and click **Apply to All**.

31. Save your presentation.

Print Your Presentation

32. Choose **File→Print** to display the Print tab in Backstage view.

33. Use the scroll bar at the right of the PowerPoint window to navigate the slides until slide 3, Increased Literacy, displays.

34. Choose your printer from the **Printer** option. Your instructor may prefer you to choose the PDF option.

35. Opt to print only the current slide; opt to print full-page slides, one slide per page.

36. Set the color option to **Grayscale**; print one copy.

37. Exit PowerPoint.

Create a Presentation from a Word Outline

In this exercise, you will import a Word outline to create the initial slides for a Kids for Change community presentation. You will then reset the slide formatting and arrange the slides into sections to make the presentation both more visually appealing and easier for you to manage. Finally, you will print a slide.

1. Start PowerPoint, click **Blank Presentation**, and save your file as **P2-R3-Outline** to your file storage location.

2. Choose **Design→Themes→Retrospect** to apply that design theme.

3. Choose **Home→Slides→New Slide menu button ▼→Slides from Outline** to begin importing a Word outline.

4. Navigate to your **PowerPoint Chapter 2** folder and double-click the **P2-R3-Outline** Word document to import the outline and create the slides.

5. Select slide 1 in the Slides panel and tap ⌷Delete⌷ to delete the blank slide.

6. Choose **Home→Slides→Layout menu button ▼→Title Slide** to change the layout of the first slide.

7. Click slide 1 in the Slides panel to ensure it is selected, scroll to the bottom of the Slides panel, and ⌷Shift⌷+click the final slide (slide 6) so that all slides are selected.

8. Choose **Home→Slides→Reset** to reset the formatting of all slides.

Create Additional Slides

9. Choose **View→Presentation Views→Outline View**.

10. Locate the Bully No More slide in the Outline panel.

11. Click to the right of the word *programs* in the last paragraph of the **Bully No More** slide in the Outline panel.

12. Tap ⌷Ctrl⌷+⌷Enter⌷ to create a slide.

13. Type **Kids for Change** in the Outline panel as the slide title, tap ⌷Enter⌷, and then tap ⌷Tab⌷ to create a new, bulleted paragraph.

14. Type **Part of the Solution** in the Outline panel.

15. Choose **Home→Slides→Layout ▼→Section Header**.

Copy Formatting

16. Choose **View→Presentation Views→Normal**.

17. Display slide 4, **Toy Collection**.

18. Select the text *foster homes*.

19. Choose **Home→Font→Bold**.

20. Double-click the **Home→Clipboard→Format Painter** button to load the Format Painter for multiple uses.

21. Click each of the words *emergency*, *responders*, *Child*, and *Services* to copy the bold formatting.

22. Choose **Home→Clipboard→Format Painter** to unload the Format Painter.

Add Slide and Handout Footers

23. Choose **View→Master Views→Handout Master**.

24. Click in the top-left placeholder and type `Kids for Change`.

25. Click in the bottom-left placeholder and type `A presentation by [Your Name]`.

26. Choose **Handout Master→Close→Close Master View**.

27. Choose **Insert→Text→Header & Footer**.

28. Check the box for **Slide Number**.

29. Check the box for **Footer** and type `A Kids for Change Presentation` in the footer box.

30. Check the box for **Don't Show on Title Slide** and click **Apply to All**.

Organize the Presentation

31. Choose **View→Presentation Views→Slide Sorter**.

32. Slide the **Zoom** slider at the bottom right of the PowerPoint window until all seven slides are visible.

33. Click the **iRecycling Day** slide to select it.

34. Choose **Home→Slides→Section menu button** ▼ **→Add Section** to create a new section.

35. Right-click the untitled section heading and choose **Rename Section**.

36. Type `Community` and then click **Rename**.

37. Click the **Bully No More** slide.

38. Choose **Home→Slides→Section menu button** ▼ **→Add Section**.

39. Right-click the untitled section heading and choose **Rename Section**.

40. Type `School` and then click **Rename**.

41. Drag the **Tutoring** slide to the right of the Bully No More slide to move it to the *School* section.

42. Save the presentation.

Print Slides

43. Choose **File→Print** to display the Print tab in Backstage view.

44. Use the scroll bar at the right of the PowerPoint window to navigate the slides until slide 1 displays.

45. Choose your printer from the **Printer** option. Use the PDF option if specified by your instructor.

46. Specify to print a **Custom Range** of slides and type **1–3** in the range box.

47. Specify `3 Slides` per page.

48. Set the color option to **Pure Black and White**; print one copy.

49. Exit PowerPoint.

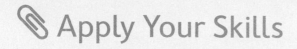 Apply Your Skills

Reformat a Presentation

In this exercise, you will create a promotional presentation for Universal Corporate Events based on a Microsoft Word outline to use during client meetings. You will then add a slide and format text so that it is consistently and professionally formatted.

1. Start Word, click **Blank Document**, and save the file as `P2-A1-Outline` in your file-saving location.

2. Choose **View→Views→Outline**.

3. Type the following text, using $\boxed{\text{Enter}}$, $\boxed{\text{Tab}}$, and $\boxed{\text{Shift}}$+$\boxed{\text{Tab}}$ as needed to create an outline in Word:

   ⊕ Universal Corporate Events
     ⊖ Events made easy
   ⊕ Event Types
     ⊖ Celebrations
     ⊖ Ceremonies
     ⊖ Team building
     ⊖ Trade shows
   ⊕ Services
     ⊖ Catering
     ⊖ Invitations
     ⊖ Stage and sound equipment
     ⊖ Venue scouting
   ⊕ Benefits
     ⊕ Our Jobs
        ⊖ Deal with paperwork
        ⊖ Guarantee safety
        ⊖ Scheduling
     ⊕ Your Jobs
        ⊖ Relax
        ⊖ Enjoy your event
   ⊕ Universal Corporate Events
     ⊖ Events made easy

4. Save and then close your file. Exit Word.

Import a Word Outline

5. Start PowerPoint, click **Blank Presentation**, and save your file as `P2-A1-Outline`.

6. Choose **Home→Slides→New Slide menu button ▼→Slides from Outline**.

7. Browse to your **P2-A1-Outline** Word outline and double-click it.

8. Delete the blank first slide.

Add a Slide

9. Display the presentation in **Outline View**.

10. Click at the end of the last paragraph of the Benefits slide in the Outline panel.

11. Press [Ctrl]+[Enter] to create a new slide.

12. Type **Specialties**, tap [Enter], and then tap [Tab].

13. Type the following paragraphs, tapping [Enter] after each except the last one:
    - `Custom catering`
    - `Individual transportation`
    - `Group transportation`
    - `Line dancing`
    - `Graphic design`
    - `Radio promotion`
    - `Emergency medical`
    - `Large-item printing`

Format the Presentation

14. Apply the **Facet** design document theme.

15. Display the presentation in **Normal** view.

16. Apply the **Title Slide** layout to the first slide.

17. Apply the **Section Header** layout to the last slide.

18. Apply the **Two Content** layout to the Specialties slide.

19. Select the last four paragraphs on the Specialties slide and move them to the new right-column placeholder.

20. Select all six slides and choose **Home→Slides→Reset**.

21. Display slide 4, **Benefits**.

22. Click anywhere in the bulleted text and then select the text box border.

23. Choose **Home→Font→Character Spacing menu button** ▼→**Loose** to spread the text out horizontally.

Use the Format Painter

24. Select the *Our Jobs* paragraph; bold the text.

25. Load the Format Painter with the formatting.

26. Drag across the *Your Jobs* paragraph to copy the formatting to the paragraph.

27. Save your presentation and exit PowerPoint.

Organize and Print a Presentation

In this exercise, you will use Slide Sorter view to create sections and organize the slides within a presentation to make it easier for you and collaborators to manage. You will then print a portion of the presentation so that you can proof audience handouts.

1. Start PowerPoint. Open **P2-A2-Outline** from the **PowerPoint Chapter 2** folder and save it as **P2-A2-OutlineRevised**.
2. Display the presentation in **Slide Sorter** view.
3. Drag the **Zoom** slider in the lower-right area of the PowerPoint window until you can see all six slides.

Rearrange Slides and Add Sections

4. Drag the **Benefits** slide so that it is after the Specialties slide.
5. Drag the **Services** slide so that it is before the Event Types slide.
6. Click the **Services** slide and then add a section named **Services**.
7. Click the **Benefits** slide and then add a section named **Closing**.

Add Slide and Handout Footers

8. Display the **Handout Master** tab.
9. Click in the bottom-left placeholder and type **UCE Promo**.
10. Click the **Close Master View** button.
11. Add the slide number and date and set to update automatically all slides except the title slide.
12. Save your presentation.

Print a Presentation

13. Choose **File→Print**.
14. Using the **Grayscale** option, print handouts with two slides per page. Print the slide as a PDF file if directed to do so by your instructor.
15. Close the presentation and exit PowerPoint.

Create, Format, and Organize a Presentation

In this exercise, you will create and import an outline from Word and then design and format a presentation.

1. Start Word and use **Outline View** to create an outline that will produce the following slides:

Title	Bullets
Universal Corporate Events	Specialized
Specialties	Custom catering
	Individual transportation
	Group transportation
	Line dancing
	Graphic design
	Radio promotion
	Emergency medical
	Large-item printing
Catering	Vegan dishes
	Kosher dishes
	Meat-lovers dishes
	Desserts
Transportation	Individual limos
	Group buses for 6–50
Line Dancing	Experienced dance leaders
	Country, pop, and hip-hop
Graphic Design	Invitation graphics
	Signs
	Banners
Radio Promotion	Script writing
	Voice talent
	High-definition recording
Emergency Medical	CPR-certified staff
	Onsite portable defibrillators
Large-Item Printing	Canvas, polyester, or vinyl
	Up to 64 square feet

2. Save the outline to your file storage location as **P2-A3-Outline** and close Word.

3. Start PowerPoint and create a new, blank presentation in your file storage location named **P2-A3-Outline**.

4. Import the **P2-A3-Outline** Word outline.

5. Delete the blank first slide.

Work with Slides and Formatting

6. Select all slides in the Slides panel and use the **Reset** command to reset the formatting.

7. Apply the **Ion Boardroom** theme and apply the orange variation.

8. Change the layout of the first slide to **Title Slide**.

9. Change the layout of the second slide to **Two Content**.

10. Move the last four paragraphs of the second slide into the new right-column placeholder.

11. Increase the line spacing of both columns on slide 2 to **2.0**.

12. Display the **Catering** slide.

13. Make the word *Vegan* bold and italic and then use the **Format Painter** to copy the formatting to the words *Kosher* and *Meat-lovers*.

14. Change the case of all eight paragraphs on the **Specialties** slide to **Capitalize Each Word**.

Work with an Outline

15. Display the presentation in **Outline View**.

16. Collapse all the slides on the Outline panel.

17. Expand only the **Specialties** slide in the Outline panel.

    Collapsing all but one slide reduces the clutter in the Outline panel and makes it easier to focus your attention on the single expanded slide.

18. In the Outline panel, locate the Specialties slide and move the *Large-item printing* paragraph below the *Graphic design* paragraph.

19. In the Outline panel, move the **Large-Item Printing** slide below the Graphic Design slide.

Organize Slides

20. Display the presentation in **Slide Sorter** view.

21. Create a new section starting with slide 1 named `Intro`.

22. Create a new section starting with the **Catering** slide named `Food and Entertainment`.

23. Create a new section starting with the **Transportation** slide named `Logistics and Emergency`.

24. Create a new section starting with the **Graphic Design** slide named `Promotion`.

25. Move the **Line Dancing** slide to the end of the *Food and Entertainment* section.

26. Move the **Emergency Medical** slide to the end of the *Logistics and Emergency* section.

27. Move the entire *Promotion* section so that it is before the *Logistics and Emergency* section.

Add Slide and Handout Footers

28. Display the **Handout Master** tab.

29. Click in the top-left placeholder and type `UCE - Event Specialists`.

30. Click in the bottom-left placeholder and type `July Presentation`.

31. Click the **Close Master View** button.

32. Add the slide number to all slides, including the title slide.

33. Save the presentation.

Print a Presentation

34. Print the slides in the *Promotion* section in the **Handouts (3 slides per page)** format so that only a single page prints. Print in **Grayscale** to save on color ink. (Or print to PDF if instructed to by your instructor.)

35. Exit PowerPoint.

⬔ Extend Your Skills

These exercises challenge you to think critically and apply your new skills. You will be evaluated on your ability to follow directions, completeness, creativity, and the use of proper grammar and mechanics. Save files to your chapter folder. Submit assignments as directed.

P2-E1   That's the Way I See It

You're teaching a cooking class and need a presentation to show others how to make your signature dish. Choose a recipe that you know well, or find one online. When you're ready, create a new presentation named **P2-E1-Recipe**.

Apply the design theme and variation of your choice. If you can't find one you like, use PowerPoint's Start screen to search for others. Type the recipe name as the slide title and create an engaging subtitle. Add a Title and Content slide that lists the ingredients. Create at least three more slides, each of which describes a few fun facts about one of the ingredients (look it up or make it up).

Add a slide that describes each step. Each paragraph should contain no more than four words. Create an additional slide for each step, using the brief description as the slide title and bulleted paragraphs to further explain the step. Create an Ingredients section that contains all the ingredient slides and a Steps section that includes all the step slides. Finally, run the slide show and make note of anything you want to change. When the slide show ends, make the changes and then save your presentation.

P2-E2   Be Your Own Boss

Open **P2-E2-BlueJean** and save it as **P2-E2-BlueJeanRevised**. View the presentation as a slide show and ask yourself if the slides are easy to read and in the best order. Based on your evaluation, use the skills taught in this lesson to make the necessary changes, ensuring that you cover these edits:

▶ Change the document theme

▶ Rearrange the order of slides

▶ Adjust the text layout

▶ Edit text

Be sure the design and formatting are consistent from slide to slide. Add at least three more slides, such as those to describe Blue Jean Landscaping products, a brief company history, or a price list. Rearrange the slides and create at least two sections to group slides in a logical order.

P2-E3   Demonstrate Proficiency

Stormy BBQ is sponsoring a Father's Day picnic. Create a PowerPoint presentation to display on the widescreen monitors at the restaurant to play during business hours that gives details about the event. Create an outline in Word, saved as **P2-E3-FathersDay**, that will produce at least five slides when imported into PowerPoint. The slides should describe the picnic and various events and entertainment.

Import the outline into PowerPoint to create the initial slides. Use an appropriate theme and change the slide layouts as necessary. Format the text so important words stand out, but be careful not to overdo it! Experiment with character and line spacing, paragraph alignment, and other formatting. Create sections for different parts of the event, such as for food, games, and other activities. Save your final presentation as **P2-E3-FathersDay**.

3
Adding Graphics, Animation, and Sound

In this chapter, you will enhance a presentation that currently includes only text. You will use pictures to add interest to the presentation, drawing objects to add spark, and slide transitions and animations to "bring the presentation to life."

LEARNING OBJECTIVES

▸ Add pictures, screenshots, and shapes to a presentation

▸ Remove backgrounds and apply artistic effects to slide images

▸ Add transition effects to a slide show

▸ Add animation to objects on a slide

▸ Add sound effects to transitions and animations

Project: Adding Eye Candy

The iJams presentation is evolving nicely. However, you know you will have to add some pizzazz to it if iJams is to contend with its competitors. Although you have created an error-free, technically perfect presentation, you can see that something is definitely missing! You decide that, if used sparingly, pictures and animation will enhance the presentation.

Working with Online Pictures

You can search for and insert pictures from the Internet directly from within PowerPoint. Adding pictures will help you emphasize key points and add polish to the presentation as a whole.

Microsoft uses the term *pictures* to refer to a range of graphic elements, including clip art and photographs. The term *clip art* is an industry-standard term referring to pre-drawn artwork that is added to computer documents. Searching for pictures from within PowerPoint displays results including both clip art and photographs.

Obeying Copyright Law

As per U.S. copyright law, it is illegal to use copyrighted pictures without the express consent of the copyright owner. This means you cannot simply search the Internet and use any picture you happen to find, as that picture may be protected by copyright. However, PowerPoint uses the Bing search engine to search for pictures online and by default displays only pictures licensed under Creative Commons, meaning you can use these pictures freely in your presentations.

Point to any picture in the search results to display its source information and size.

Clicking this button causes PowerPoint to display all results—even those that are copyrighted and therefore illegal to use without express permission.

 Using copyrighted pictures without permission can result in a lawsuit or fines of several thousand dollars.

Using Text and Object Layouts

PowerPoint creates slides with different layouts, such as slides with titles only and slides with titles and text. These slide layouts allow you to easily create slides with a standardized title and bulleted text. Many of PowerPoint's layouts, including the Title and Content layout and the Two Content layout, provide placeholders for titles, text, and various types of content including tables, charts, pictures from the Internet or your computer, organizational charts, and videos.

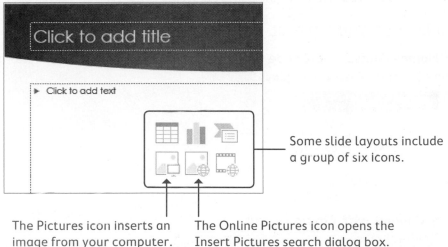

Some slide layouts include a group of six icons.

The Pictures icon inserts an image from your computer.

The Online Pictures icon opens the Insert Pictures search dialog box.

SLIDE INSERT SHORTCUTS

Icon	What It Does	Icon	What It Does	Icon	What It Does
	Inserts a table		Inserts a chart or graph		Inserts a SmartArt graphic
	Inserts a picture from your computer		Opens the Online Pictures dialog box		Inserts a video clip from your computer or online

Deleting Placeholder Text

You may decide to replace all text on a slide with a graphic. Deleting all text inside a placeholder results in the slide displaying its six default insert icons, making it easy to insert a picture or other objects.

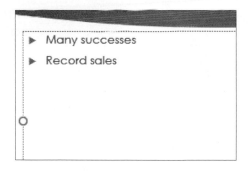

When all the text inside a placeholder is deleted...

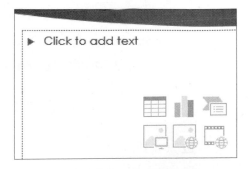

...the six insert icons reappear.

In this exercise, you will get a slide ready to accept a picture.

1. Start PowerPoint. Open **P3-D1-Animation** from the **PowerPoint Chapter 3** folder and save it as `P3-D1-AnimationRevised`.
2. Select the **Our Services** slide from the Slides panel.

Choose a Layout and Format Text

3. Choose **Home→Slides→New Slide menu button ▼**. Be sure to click the bottom half of the New Slide button so the menu displays.

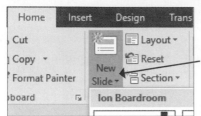

4. Select the **Content with Caption** layout.

   A new slide is inserted below Our Services *and has the Content with Caption layout applied in a single step. Using this method is faster than first adding a new slide and then changing its layout in a second step.*

5. In the Title placeholder, type `Our Recent Success`.
6. In the text box beneath the title, type:

   `Top of the Rock` Enter

   `Excellence in Service to Musicians` Enter

   `League of Electronic Music Distributors`

7. Select the text *Top of the Rock* and choose **Home→Font→Font Size menu button ▼→24**.
8. Choose **Home→Font→Bold**.
9. Select the text *League of Electronic Music Distributors*.
10. Choose **Home→Font→Italic**.
11. Click in the large text placeholder at the right and type:

    `Many successes` Enter

    `Record-breaking sales`

    As soon as you start typing, the six slide icons disappear. You decide instead to replace the bulleted text with a picture. You will delete all the text in the placeholder so the slide displays the six insert icons again.

12. Click inside the text box, if necessary, to display its dashed border.
13. Click the dashed border to select the text box.
14. Tap Delete.

    The text is deleted, and the six insert icons reappear.

15. Save your presentation.

Searching for Pictures with the Insert Pictures Search Window

The Insert Pictures search window lets you search for pictures on the Internet using the Bing search engine. You can also search Facebook, Flickr, and other sites if you are signed in to your Microsoft account.

 View the video "The Insert Pictures Search Window."

≡ Insert a picture from an online source: Insert→Images→Online Pictures  or click Online Pictures on the slide

≡ Insert a picture from your computer: Insert→Images→Pictures or click Pictures on the slide

---

DEVELOP YOUR SKILLS: P3-D2

In this exercise, you will insert a picture to add visual interest to a slide.

1. Save your file as **P3-D2-AnimationRevised**.
2. On the **Our Recent Success** slide, click the **Online Pictures** icon to open the Insert Pictures search window.
3. Type **award** in the Bing Image Search box and tap Enter.
4. Follow these steps to insert a picture on the slide:

Ⓐ Scroll until you find any award picture you like. Your results may differ from the figure.

Ⓑ Click the desired picture to select it.

Ⓒ Click **Insert**.

 If you don't like the picture when you see it in the slide, tap Delete and then start this exercise over at step 2 to try a different picture.

The picture is inserted on the slide and replaces the large text box.

5. Save the presentation.

Moving, Sizing, and Rotating Objects

When you click an object (such as a picture), sizing handles and a rotate handle appear. You can easily move, size, and rotate the selected object so that it fits perfectly on the slide.

You can resize objects to be wider or taller than their original size to better fit a slide's contents. If you want to maintain the original picture proportions, take care to drag the handles in the four corners of the picture only. Similarly, you can rotate a picture by dragging the rotate handle, which looks like a circular arrow, left or right. Rotating a picture sets it at an angle.

 Remember that to manipulate the size or rotation of an object, you must select it first.

Objects can be moved around the slide as you like. When moving, it's not necessary to select the object first, though. Hovering the mouse pointer over the picture will change it to a four-headed arrow. That arrow means the object is ready to be moved.

 View the video "Manipulating Objects."

Stacking Objects

Sometimes when you insert a picture, it overlaps text or some other object(s). You can change the stacking order of objects, such as pictures and shapes, by moving them forward or backward.

If an object is covering text...　　　　　　　...send it behind the text.

☰ Move by one object at a time: Picture Tools→Format→Arrange→Send Backward ⬚ *or* Bring Forward ⬚

☰ Move to front/back: Picture Tools→Format→Arrange→Send Backward ⬚ menu button ▼→ Send to Back ⬚ *or* Bring Forward ⬚ menu button ▼→Bring to Front ⬚

In this exercise, you will manipulate a picture, sizing and moving it to place it on the slide.

1. Save your file as **P3-D3-AnimationRevised**.

2. Follow these steps to rotate the picture:

Ⓐ Point to the rotate handle until the insertion point changes to a circular arrow.

Ⓑ Press the left mouse button and drag slowly to the right. Release the mouse button after the image has rotated about 90 degrees.

Ⓒ Choose **Quick Access Toolbar→Undo**.

3. Follow these steps to resize the picture:

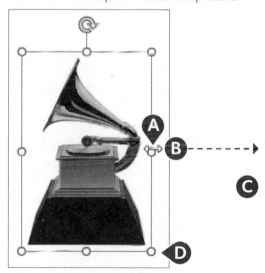

Ⓐ Point to the handle on the right side so the insertion point becomes a double-headed arrow.

Ⓑ Press the left mouse button and drag right until the image is twice as wide as the original and stretched too wide.

Ⓒ Choose **Quick Access Toolbar→Undo**.

Ⓓ Point to a bottom-right corner handle so the mouse becomes a double-headed arrow and drag to enlarge the image proportionately to your liking.

4. Point to the image itself (not the border or a resize handle) until the pointer becomes a four-headed arrow. Drag so the image is centered next to the bar of text.

Compare your slide with the following illustration.

5. Save your presentation.

Formatting Pictures

After your picture is on the slide, use the various groups on the contextual Format tab to add effects or align your picture. You can add borders, drop shadows, or bevels, or rotate your picture in 3-D from the Picture Styles group on the Format tab. Other groups on this tab allow you to align, flip, crop, or perform basic image-editing tasks.

☰ Picture Tools→Format→Picture Styles

DEVELOP YOUR SKILLS: P3-D4

In this exercise, you will work with the Ribbon to insert and format a music-related picture on your slide.

1. Save your file as **P3-D4-AnimationRevised**.
2. Display the title slide.
3. Choose **Insert→Images→Online Pictures** .
4. Type **music cd** in the Bing Image Search box and tap [Enter].
5. Scroll through the results. When you find a suitable picture, select it and click **Insert**.

   A suitable picture is one that is high quality and that an audience can recognize when viewing a slide show from across a room.

Size and Position the Picture

6. Click the picture on the slide to display its border, drag the corner handles to resize the picture proportionally, and then drag the picture to fit in the space above the text. Be sure the picture does not overlap the text.

7. Choose **Picture Tools→Format→Arrange→Align menu button ▼→Align Center**.

    Selecting a picture forces the display of the contextual Format tab.

8. Make sure the picture displays handles to indicate that it is selected and then choose **Picture Tools→Format→Picture Styles→Picture Effects menu button ▼**.

9. Roll your insertion point over several of the items in the Picture Effects gallery to view a Live Preview of each effect.

    As you have seen with other commands, Live Preview makes it easy to anticipate the effect of a command without the need to undo it if you don't like the effect.

10. Choose **Format→Picture Styles→Picture Effects→Glow→Gold, 18 pt Glow, Accent Color 3**.

    PowerPoint applies a glowing effect to the edge of the image.

11. If necessary, resize and move your image so it doesn't overlap the text.

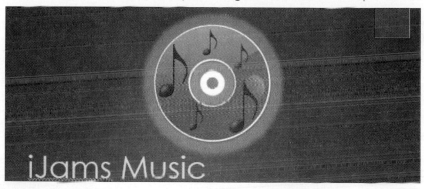

12. Save your presentation.

Adding Other Graphics

Sometimes you just can't find that perfect picture through PowerPoint's online search. Often you can incorporate more unique and personal imagery if you take your own pictures or download professional photographs from a commercial website. PowerPoint includes tools and features to make the most of your pictures, including the ability to remove a background and add artistic effects.

Removing a Background

Many times a photograph contains more than what you need. In the past, it was necessary to use a graphics-editing program to remove the background or other unwanted elements. PowerPoint includes a feature that allows you to remove backgrounds with just a few clicks. When removing a background, the original picture is not harmed, because PowerPoint works on a copy of the picture embedded in the slide. Additionally, nothing is actually removed from the picture. PowerPoint just hides areas of the picture that you mark to be removed. The hidden areas can always be made visible again. You can adjust the settings of the removal tool at any time after the background's initial removal using the Mark Areas to Keep and Mark Areas to Remove commands, so there is no need to worry about getting it perfect on your first try.

The Background Removal tool overlays in purple the areas to be removed.

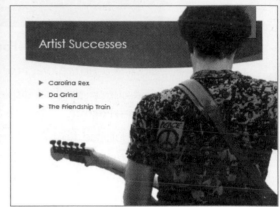

With just a few clicks, the background can be removed.

 Picture Tools→Format→Adjust→Remove Background

DEVELOP YOUR SKILLS: P3-D5

In this exercise, you will insert a picture and remove the background.

1. Save your file as **P3-D5-AnimationRevised**.
2. Scroll down the Slides panel, if necessary, and select the **Artist Successes** slide.
3. Choose **Insert→Images→Pictures**.
4. Navigate to your **PowerPoint Chapter 3** folder, select the **P3-D5-Guitarist** picture, and click **Insert**.

   The picture is inserted on the slide but contains more imagery than we need.

Remove the Background

5. Drag the picture up so its top snaps to the top of the slide.
6. Drag the bottom-left corner handle down and left until the bottom of the picture snaps to the bottom of the slide.

   Dragging a corner handle maintains the proportions of the picture so it doesn't appear stretched or distorted. The picture now covers the whole slide. The left part of the picture extends off the slide and will be cut off during a slide show. This is preferable to dragging the picture taller out of proportion and having it fit the slide exactly.

7. Choose **Picture Tools→Format→Adjust→Remove Background**.

PowerPoint places a rectangular border inside the picture and does its best to guess what you want to remove. A purple overlay indicates the content that will be removed. You will adjust this.

8. Drag the top-right handle of the rectangular box inside the picture so it snaps to the top-right corner of the picture.

9. Drag the bottom-left handle of the rectangular box down and right so the entire guitar is inside the box and the bottom border snaps to the bottom of the picture.

Your slide should resemble the following image, but it will not be exact.

When you resize the box inside the picture, PowerPoint adjusts the purple overlay. The overlay still needs to be adjusted so you can see the whole guitarist.

10. Choose **Background Removal→Refine→Mark Areas to Keep**.

11. Follow these steps to adjust the overlay:

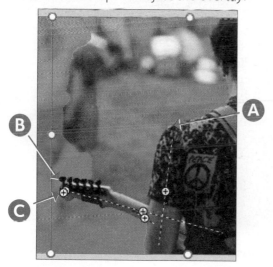

Ⓐ Point to the top of the left shoulder and drag down to the bottom of the elbow to tell PowerPoint not to remove this area.

Ⓑ Point to the left edge of the guitar and drag right to keep this area.

Ⓒ Drag over any other purple on the guitarist or the guitar.

12. Choose **Background Removal→Refine→Mark Areas to Remove**.

13. Follow these steps to define areas to be removed:

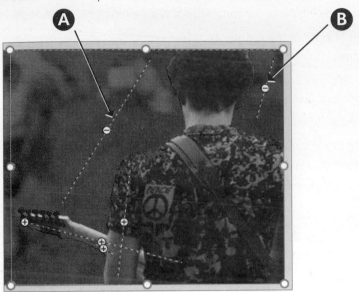

Ⓐ Drag over the background to tell PowerPoint to remove this area.

Ⓑ Drag over this section to remove it as well.

You will probably have to go back and forth with the Mark Areas to Keep and Mark Areas to Remove buttons as you continue to tweak the purple overlay. Be sure no part of the guitarist's shirt is purple. You may want to also remove the small spaces to the left and right of the guitarist's body.

14. Choose **Background Removal→Close→Keep Changes**.

15. Drag the image to the right so that the red ribbon at the top of the slide is covered by the picture.

16. If your slide doesn't resemble the figure, choose **Picture Tools→Format→Adjust→Remove Background** to adjust the overlay.

Parts of the picture extend to both the left and right beyond the slide. While it may look strange in Normal view, it will look fine as a slide show. The areas outside the slide will not display.

17. Save your presentation.

Applying Artistic Effects

PowerPoint includes artistic effects that can be applied to pictures, making photographs look like pencil sketches, cement, or pastels. Additionally, pictures can be recolored to create a color cast that blends with your theme.

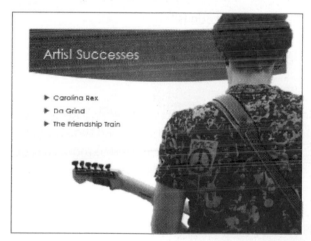

No effects have been applied.

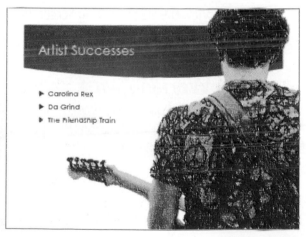

Pencil Sketch and Recolor effects have been applied.

 Picture Tools→Format→Adjust→Artistic Effects

In this exercise, you will apply artistic effects to a picture to enhance its visual appeal.

1. Save your file as **P3-D6-AnimationRevised**.
2. If necessary, select the picture on the sixth slide, **Artistic Successes**.
3. Choose **Picture Tools→Format→Adjust→Artistic Effects menu button** ▼.
4. Point to several effects to see how they change the picture on the slide. Notice that a ToolTip appears when you point to an effect, indicating its name.
5. Select the **Pencil Grayscale** effect.
6. Choose **Picture Tools→Format→Adjust→Color**.
7. Point to several color adjustments to see how they change the picture on the slide.
   Notice the ToolTips that appear.
8. Select the **Recolor→Teal, Accent Color 5 Light** adjustment.
9. Save your presentation.

Inserting a Screenshot

You may want to include a picture of something on your computer screen, such as a program window or web page, in a presentation. PowerPoint's Screenshot tool lets you insert a picture of any open window or program or drag on your screen to define an area to insert. You can insert either a full program or folder window, or take a screenshot of a portion of a window.

 View the video "Adding Screenshots from Other Applications."

≡ Insert→Images→Screenshot 📷 menu button ▼

Working with Shapes

PowerPoint offers more than 150 shapes that you can add to your slides. You can use these shapes to build your own custom flowcharts, mathematical equations, speech and thought bubbles, or other designs. Shapes can even include text—and they are all preformatted to match a slide's theme.

≡ Insert→Illustrations→Shapes ⬚

Stretching a Shape

You can stretch shapes to make them wider/narrower or taller/shorter. All shapes are preformatted with a specific ratio of width to height, so stretching a shape can sometimes make it appear unbalanced. Whenever possible, you should maintain the original aspect ratio, as a distorted shape makes a slide appear amateurish.

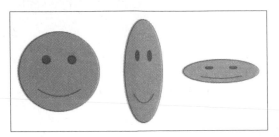

The original proportions are balanced (left), but stretching the shape may cause it to look distorted and amateurish.

Adding Text to a Shape

You can easily add text to a shape, but the text does not automatically resize itself to fit nicely. Text will, however, automatically wrap to the next line, so there is no need to tap [Enter] as you type.

Text automatically wraps to the next line but does not automatically get smaller to fit inside the shape. You may need to adjust the text size to get it to fit.

Formatting Shapes and Shape Text

While shapes and the text they contain are automatically formatted to match the slide's theme, you may want a more exciting look such as a drop-shadow or 3-D effect. Adding a Shape style or WordArt style can make your shape graphics really pop.

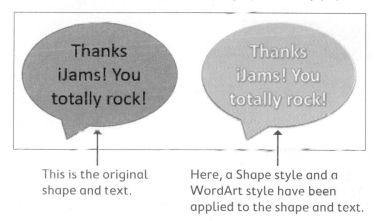

This is the original shape and text.

Here, a Shape style and a WordArt style have been applied to the shape and text.

Shape Variations

When selected on a slide, some shapes display a yellow handle that you can use to change the shape's properties. For example, you can change the Smiley Face shape to a frown.

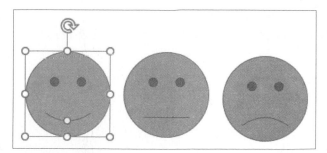

Dragging the yellow handle generates shape variations.

Merging Shapes

If you need a shape that PowerPoint doesn't offer, you can merge shapes to generate your own custom shape. The benefit of this is that your new custom shape has a single outline and truly looks like a single shape rather than several overlapped shapes.

 View the video "Custom Shapes."

DEVELOP YOUR SKILLS: P3-D7

In this exercise, you will use a shape to emphasize important slide text.

1. Save your file as **P3-D7-AnimationRevised**.

2. Display the seventh slide, **Carolina Rex**.

3. Choose **Insert→Illustrations→Shapes menu button ▼→Stars and Banners→ 5-Point Star**.

4. Hold ⎡Shift⎤ as you drag on the slide to create a star shape that fills most of the white area to the right of the text. Make sure the shape does not extend into the top colored part of the slide.

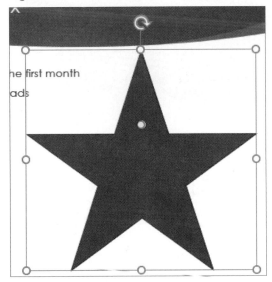

5. Type **Top Seller!** in the shape.

Your star shape should resemble this figure, though your text may span two lines.

6. Click the dashed border of the shape so it turns solid.

When the shape is selected, you can format its text.

7. Choose **Home→Font→Font Size menu button ▼→54**.

The font size increases, but the text no longer fits nicely inside the shape. You will fix this in the next few steps.

Customize the Shape

8. Follow these steps to change the shape of the star and make the text fit nicely:

A Drag the yellow handle up a little bit to change the shape of the star.

B Try to match your star shape to the figure. You may have to drag the yellow handle up or down.

Format the Shape and Text

9. Choose **Drawing Tools→Format→Shape Styles→More ▼→Theme Styles→Intense Effect – Purple, Accent 6**.

The shape changes color and appears three-dimensional. However, the text remains the same.

10. Choose **Drawing Tools→Format→WordArt Styles→More ▼→Fill – White, Outline – Accent 5, Shadow**.

The text within the shape changes.

11. If necessary, change the size of the star shape so the text fits on two lines.

12. Save your presentation.

Working with Slide Transitions

A slide transition is the animation between slides. Used properly, these transitions can add zest and excitement to your presentation and provide a distinct breaking point between slides. PowerPoint includes many transitions that are often used in video production, such as 3-D rotations and other animated effects.

 View the video "Slide Transitions."

 Consistency within a presentation helps keep the audience focused. Avoid using different transitions within a single presentation.

Creating Transitions in Slide Sorter View

Most of the time, you will want to apply the same transition to the entire presentation. Maintaining a consistent transition style looks more professional (less haphazard) and is less distracting for the audience. Using the Slide Sorter view is a quick and easy way to apply transitions, as you can see all slide thumbnails at the same time. You can apply transitions to a single slide, multiple slides, or all slides in a presentation. Transitions animate the change from one slide to another, not individual elements of the slide. The Transitions tab on the Ribbon contains commands to apply transitions, as well as sound, duration, and other options.

≡ Transitions→Transition to This Slide

DEVELOP YOUR SKILLS: P3-D8

In this exercise, you will apply a transition to all slides except the title slide to make the slide show more interesting.

1. Save your file as **P3-D8-AnimationRevised**.
2. Choose **View→Presentation Views→Slide Sorter**.
3. Press Ctrl + A to select all slides.
4. Ctrl +click on the **first slide** to remove it from the selection.

   Slides 2–11 are selected.
5. Choose **Transitions→Transition to This Slide→More** ▾ and locate the *Exciting* group.
6. Click **Vortex** to apply the transition to all selected slides.

   PowerPoint displays an animated preview of each slide transition.
7. Tap Esc to stop the transition previews.
8. Choose **Transitions→Transition to This Slide→Effect Options menu button ▼→From Top**.

   This sets the transition to animate from the top of each slide down rather than from the default setting of left to right.
9. Tap Esc to stop the transition previews.

10. Follow these steps to change the transition duration:

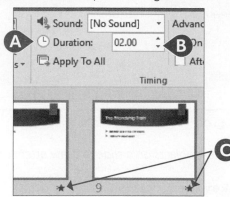

Ⓐ Locate the **Transitions→Timing→Duration** setting.

Ⓑ Click the down button repeatedly to set the duration to **02.00**.

Ⓒ Notice the star icons indicating a transition effect for the slides.

The title slide does not have the star icon because there is no transition applied to it.

Run the Presentation

11. Choose **Slide Show→Start Slide Show→From Beginning**.

The title slide appears without a transition. The title slide would have opened with the Vortex transition if you had applied the transition to it.

12. Click the mouse button to advance to the next slide.

The Vortex transition effect displays as the slides advance.

13. Continue to click the mouse button until you reach the end of the presentation and the Slide Sorter window reappears.

14. Save your presentation.

Using Slide Animation

Whereas transitions are applied to slides as a whole, animations are applied to individual objects on a slide. Animations begin only after any transition effect is completed. Some examples of animation include:

▸ A picture that moves across the slide to its final location

▸ A slide that starts out empty and then has a title and other elements that fade into view with a mouse click

▸ Bulleted paragraphs that fly in from the bottom of the slide, one by one, each time the presenter clicks with the mouse

 Less is more. Animation can distract an audience, so use it sparingly.

PowerPoint offers more than 40 animations you can add to objects on a slide by using a single command. For example, the Fade animation tells PowerPoint to gradually make objects on a slide fade into view after any transition effect is completed.

 View the video "Animations."

Setting Animation Options

After applying an animation to an object, you will likely want to set the animation options to control exactly how the animation effect works. The available options differ based on whether the animation was applied to text or an image. The options also differ based on the animation itself. Additionally, you can set timing options to control the speed of the animation.

 View the video "Customizing Animations."

≡ Animations→Animation→Effect Options

DEVELOP YOUR SKILLS: P3-D9

In this exercise, you will apply an animation to text objects on a slide to draw attention to them.

1. Save your file as **P3-D9-AnimationRevised**.
2. Choose **View→Presentation Views→Normal**.
3. Display the **Our Services** slide.
4. Click once in the bulleted text so a dashed border appears around the text box.
5. Choose **Animations→Animation→More ⊡→Entrance→Float In**.

   The animation previews, and you see each level-1 paragraph animate across the slide.
6. Choose **Animations→Animation→Effect Options menu button ▼→Float Down** to have the paragraphs animate from the top of the slide down.

   The numbers next to each bulleted paragraph indicate the order in which the animation is applied. By default, each paragraph will animate after a mouse click.
7. Choose **Slide Show→Start Slide Show→From Beginning** to start the slide show.
8. Click anywhere with the mouse to advance to the second slide.

   The transition effect animates, but no bulleted paragraph appears yet.
9. Click anywhere with the mouse.

   The first bulleted paragraph animates into view.
10. Continue clicking until all four bulleted paragraphs are visible and the slide show advances to the third slide, Our Recent Success.
11. Tap ⎡Esc⎤ to end the slide show and return to Normal view.
12. Save your presentation.

Using the Animation Pane

By using the Animation pane, you have many more choices for effects than you have in the animation menu you used previously. You can also individually set the animation for each element on a slide. When using the Animation pane, you can control the visual effects, timing, and sequencing of the animation process. For example, rather than having to click each time to display the next animated bulleted paragraph, you can set it so that the animation starts automatically after the slide transition and continues until all objects on the slide have been animated.

Budgeting Your Time

Using the Animation pane to customize each animation is a time-consuming process. Be prepared to spend a significant amount of time selecting each animated object individually and then setting its options.

 View the video "The Animation Pane."

In this exercise, you will use the Animation pane to configure the bulleted paragraphs to animate automatically after the slide transition completes. This reduces the need for you to click constantly during a slide show.

1. Save your file as **P3-D10-AnimationRevised**.

2. Display the second slide, **Our Services**.

3. Click once in the bulleted text so a dashed border appears around the text box.

4. Choose **Animations→Advanced Animation→Animation Pane**.

   The Animation pane displays on the right side of the screen.

5. Follow these steps to begin to configure the advanced animation settings:

Ⓐ Click the **menu** button ▼ to display the menu.

Ⓑ Choose **Start After Previous** so the animation begins automatically after the previous animation (in this case, the slide transition).

   Notice that the numbers next to each bulleted paragraph in the Animation pane have changed to zeros, indicating their animations all happen at the same time, automatically, after the slide transition.

6. Click the **Click to Expand Contents** bar to show each individual paragraph.

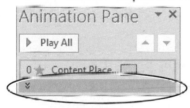

7. Follow these steps to customize the animation for the last paragraph:

Ⓐ Click once on the **Downloadable** item to display the menu button.

Ⓑ Click the **menu** button ▼ to display the menu.

Ⓒ Choose **Start with Previous** to begin this animation with the previous one (in the previous bulleted paragraph).

8. Choose **Slide Show→Start Slide Show→From Beginning**.

9. Click anywhere with the mouse to advance to the second slide.

   The bulleted paragraphs animate automatically after the slide transition ends. Each animation happens sequentially, except for the last bulleted paragraph, which animates with the previous item.

10. Tap [Esc] to end the slide show and return to Normal view.

11. Save your presentation.

Adding Sound Effects

PowerPoint provides audio clips and sound effects to accompany or accentuate your slide elements. For example, you may attach sound effects to slide transitions or animations. You can use the Transitions tab to add a sound to a slide transition or the Animation pane to add a sound to an animation.

 View the video "Sound Effects on Transitions."

≡ Transitions→Timing→Sound 🔊

Sometimes you don't want a sound effect to play during a slide transition, but rather when an animation causes an object to move across the slide.

 View the video "Sound Effects on Animations."

≡ Animations→Advanced Animation→Animation Pane 🎞

DEVELOP YOUR SKILLS: P3-D11

In this exercise, you will apply two sounds to the presentation to enhance an animation.

1. Save your file as **P3-D11-AnimationRevised**.

2. Choose the **Our Recent Success** slide and then select the picture.

3. Choose **Animations→Animation→More [▼]→Entrance→Bounce**.

4. Follow these steps to display the effect options:

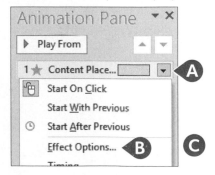

Ⓐ Click the drop-down menu for the animation.

Ⓑ Choose **Effect Options**.

Ⓒ On the Effect tab, click the **Sound menu** button ▼ and choose **Applause**.

5. Click **OK**, and the animation and sound will be previewed.

Apply a Transition Sound Effect

6. Display the **Our Services** slide.

7. Choose **Transitions→Timing→Sound→Chime**.

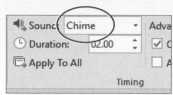

PowerPoint applies the Chime sound to the transition effect for this slide.

8. Choose **Slide Show→Start Slide Show→From Beginning**.

9. Navigate through the presentation until you hear the applause and see the Bounce animation on the Our Recent Success slide.

 You may not be able to hear the sound effect if your computer does not have speakers.

10. Press the ⌜Esc⌝ key to end the slide show early and return to Normal view.

11. Close the Animation pane.

12. Save your presentation and exit PowerPoint.

Self-Assessment

Check your knowledge of this chapter's key concepts and skills using the Self-Assessment in your ebook or eLab course.

Reinforce Your Skills

Work with Pictures

In this exercise, you will add pictures to the Kids for Change community presentation to increase interest in the group's promoted events.

1. Start PowerPoint, open **P3-R1-KidsPics** from the **PowerPoint Chapter 3** folder, and save it as **P3-R1-KidsPicsRevised**.

2. Choose the **Events** slide (second slide).

3. Choose **Home→Slides→Layout menu button ▼→Two Content**.

Insert and Format a Picture

4. Click the **Online Pictures** icon on the slide to display the Insert Pictures search window.

5. Type **calendar** in the Bing Image Search box and tap Enter.

6. Scroll through the results until you find an appropriate image.

7. Choose a picture that appeals to you and click **Insert**.

8. Drag any of the picture's corner handles to resize it so it fills the right half of the slide.

9. Drag from the center of the picture to move and position it so it does not overlap any text.

10. Drag the rotate handle above the top edge of the picture to rotate it slightly for visual interest.

11. With the picture still selected, locate the **Picture Tools→Format→Picture Styles** group of commands.

12. Point to several of the thumbnail samples in the Picture Styles gallery to preview them and then click one to apply it. Choose a style that works well with your calendar image.

Apply Advanced Image Editing Skills

13. Display the **Contact Us** slide (fourth slide).

14. Choose **Insert→Images→Pictures**.

15. Browse to your **PowerPoint Chapter 3** folder and insert the **P3-R1-Phone.jpg** picture.

16. With the picture selected on the slide, choose **Picture Tools→Format→Adjust→Remove Background**.

17. Drag the handles of the Background Removal border so the phone and wire are inside the border, and then choose **Background Removal→Close→Keep Changes**.

18. Move the phone so it is roughly centered below the phone number.

19. With the picture still selected, choose **Picture Tools→Format→Adjust→Artistic Effects→Pencil Sketch**.

20. Choose **Picture Tools→Format→Adjust→Color→Recolor→Dark Green, Accent Color 4 Light**.

21. Save the changes and exit PowerPoint.

Add Shapes and Animations

In this exercise, you will create a custom shape of a house and incorporate animation to add visual appeal to the presentation.

1. Start PowerPoint, open **P3-R2-KidsAnimated** from the **PowerPoint Chapter 3** folder, and save it as **P3-R2-KidsAnimatedRevised**.

2. Display the **This Month** slide (second slide).

3. Choose **Insert→Illustrations→Shapes menu button ▼→Rectangles→Rectangle**.

4. Drag on the slide to draw a rectangle. Resize and move it so it roughly matches this figure.

5. Choose **Insert→Illustrations→Shapes menu button ▼→Basic Shapes→Isosceles Triangle**.

6. Drag on the slide to draw a triangle to act as the roof of the house, resizing and moving it so it roughly matches the figure in step 8.

7. Choose **Insert→Illustrations→Shapes menu button ▼→Rectangles→Rectangle**.

8. Drag on the slide to draw a small rectangle to act as a chimney, resizing and moving it to roughly match this figure.

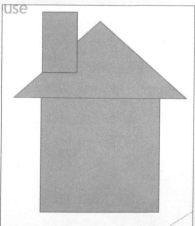

Merge Shapes

9. Click the large rectangle on the slide to select it and then use ⎡Shift⎤+click on both the triangular roof and the small chimney so that all three shapes are selected.

10. Choose **Drawing Tools→Format→Insert Shapes→Merge Shapes** ⊘ **menu button** ▼→ **Union**.

11. Choose **Insert→Illustrations→Shapes menu button** ▼→**Rectangles→Rectangle**.

12. Drag on the slide to draw a rectangle to act as the door; adjust as necessary to roughly match this figure.

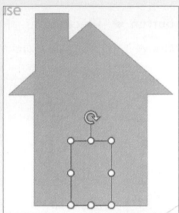

13. Click the door shape to select it, if necessary, and then use ⎡Shift⎤+click on the house so both shapes are selected.

14. Choose **Drawing Tools→Format→Insert Shapes→Merge Shapes** ⊘→**Combine**.

Format and Add Text to a Shape

15. Click the house shape to ensure it is selected and its border displays.

16. Type **Home** ⎡Enter⎤ **Sweet** ⎡Enter⎤ **Home** ⎡Enter⎤.

17. Click the shape's dashed border to select it.

18. Choose **Home→Font→Font Size menu button** ▼→**36**.

If your text no longer fits in the shape, choose a smaller font size or adjust the size of the house shape.

19. Choose **Drawing Tools→Format→Shape Styles→More** ⎡▼⎤→**Theme Styles→Intense Effect — Blue, Accent 2** (the bottom thumbnail in the third column).

20. Resize and move the shape so it fits in the upper-right area of the slide; adjust the font size as necessary.

Apply Transition Effects

21. Select slide 2, **This Month**, in the Slides panel.

22. Use Shift+click on the last slide in the Slides panel so all but the title slide are selected.

23. Choose **Transitions→Transition to This Slide→More ▼→Subtle→Random Bars**.

Add Animation

24. Display the **This Month** slide (second slide), if necessary, and then click the house shape to select it.

25. Choose **Animations→Animation→More ▼→Entrance→Bounce**.

26. Choose **Animations→Timing→Start menu button ▼→After Previous**.

27. Click the up arrow on the Delay box four times to set the delay to **1 second**.

28. Display the **Event Benefits** slide (third slide).

29. Click in any text in the left column so a dashed border appears around the text box.

30. Choose **Animations→Animation→More→Entrance→Float In**.

31. Click in any of the text in the right column so a dashed border appears around the text box.

32. Choose **Animations→Animation→More→Entrance→Float In**.

33. Choose **Animations→Advanced Animation→Animation Pane**.

34. Click the double arrows to expand the top group of content in the Animation pane.

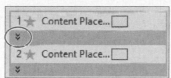

35. Click the second item, **Homeless families**, to display its menu button.

36. Click the item's **menu** button ▼ and choose **Start After Previous**.

37. Click the third item, **$0 mortgage**, to display its menu button.

38. Click the item's **menu** button ▼ and choose **Start After Previous**.

39. Click the fourth item, **A fresh start**, to display its menu button.

40. Click the item's **menu** button ▼ and choose **Start After Previous**.

41. Expand the second group's contents and set each item to **Start After Previous**.

Add a Sound Effect to an Animation

42. Display the **This Month** slide (second slide).

43. Click the **house shape** to select it.

44. Click the single item in the Animation pane, click its **menu** button ▼, and choose **Effect Options**.

45. Set the Sound menu to **Whoosh** and then click **OK**.

46. Close the Animation pane.

47. Choose **Slide Show→Start Slide Show→From Beginning** and click each slide until the slide show ends and you return to Normal view.

48. Save the changes and then exit PowerPoint.

Add Visual Interest

In this exercise, you will add pictures and animation to enhance a presentation and inspire audience members to donate to the group's toy drive.

1. Start PowerPoint, open **P3-R3-KidsVisual** from the **PowerPoint Chapter 3** folder, and save it as **P3-R3-KidsVisualRevised**.

2. Display the third slide.

3. Choose **Home→Slides→Layout menu button ▼→Two Content**.

Insert Pictures

4. Click the **Pictures** icon on the slide to insert a picture from your computer.

5. Browse to your **PowerPoint Chapter 3** folder and insert the **P3-R3-Girl.jpg** picture.

6. Drag the picture to roughly fill the right side of the slide.

7. Display the fourth slide and choose **Home→Slides→Layout menu button ▼→Two Content**.

8. Click the **Pictures** icon on the slide to insert a picture from your computer, browse to your **PowerPoint Chapter 3** folder, and insert the **P3-R3-Truck.jpg** picture.

9. Drag the truck picture to roughly center it on the slide.

10. Display the fifth slide and choose **Insert→Images→Online Pictures**.

11. Type **toy** in the Bing Image Search box and tap Enter.

12. Scroll through the results until you find a toy you like and then click the toy to select it.

13. Continue to scroll and look for more toys. Click on additional toys to add them to your selection. After you have selected six toys, click **Insert**.

Move, Size, and Rotate Pictures

14. Click an empty area of the slide to deselect the inserted pictures.

15. Click one of the toys on the slide to select it.

16. Drag a corner handle on the picture's border to make the picture smaller.

17. Drag the rotate handle above the top edge of the picture to slightly rotate it.

18. Drag the picture to move it to a position of your liking.

19. Resize, rotate, and move the remaining toys so they are spaced throughout the slide.

    Do not be concerned if the picture backgrounds overlap each other or the slide text at this point.

Remove a Background

20. Display slide 4, click the truck picture, and choose **Picture Tools→Format→Adjust→Remove Background**.

21. Drag the handles of the background removal border until the truck fits inside it.

22. Choose **Background Removal→Refine→Mark Areas to Remove**.

23. Drag on the light-colored areas on the ground near the tires to remove them.

24. Choose **Background Removal→Close→Keep Changes**.

25. Drag a corner handle of the truck's border to enlarge it and then drag the truck to position it next to the text.

26. Display slide 5; remove the pictures' backgrounds, if necessary, so they can be overlapped; and then drag the pictures to reposition them to your liking.

Format Pictures

27. Display the third slide and click the picture of the girl and her teddy bear.

28. Choose **Picture Tools→Format→Picture Styles→More→Rotated, White**.

29. Drag the picture to reposition it, if necessary.

30. With the picture of the girl and her teddy bear still selected, choose **Picture Tools→Format→ Adjust→Artistic Effects menu button ▼→Glow, Diffused**.

Add and Format a Shape with Text

31. Choose **Insert→Illustrations→Shapes menu button ▼→Stars and Banners→Up Ribbon**.

32. Use Shift +drag to create a proportional ribbon that fills the left side of the slide under the text.

33. Type **My 1st toy**.

34. Click the blue ribbon shape to select it and tap Ctrl + C to copy the shape.

35. Display the fourth slide with the truck.

36. Tap Ctrl + V to paste the shape.

37. Drag the truck picture so the blue ribbon doesn't overlap it.

38. Click the blue ribbon shape and then choose **Drawing Tools→Format→Shape Styles→Shape Effects menu button ▼→Reflection→Reflection Variations→Half Reflection, Touching**.

39. Choose **Home→Clipboard→Format Painter** to copy the formatting.

40. Display the third slide and click the blue ribbon to duplicate the shape's effect.

Apply Transition Effects

41. Choose **View→Presentation Views→Slide Sorter**.

42. Click slide 2 and then Shift +click on slide 5 so all but the title slide are selected.

43. Choose **Transitions→Transition to This Slide→More→Exciting→Glitter**.

44. Choose **Transitions→Transition to This Slide→Effect Options menu button ▼→Diamonds from Top** and click the down arrow as necessary to set the duration to **02.00**.

Apply an Animation

45. Double-click slide 5 to display it in Normal view.

46. Click one of the toys on the slide and then choose **Animations→Animation→More→ Entrance→Grow & Turn**.

47. Click a second toy on the slide to select it.

48. Choose **Animations→Animation→More→Entrance→Grow & Turn**.

49. One at a time, click each remaining toy and apply the **Grow & Turn** animation.

Use the Animation Pane

50. Choose **Animations→Advanced Animation→Animation Pane**.

51. Click the first animated item in the **Animation** pane to display its menu button ▼.

52. Click the **menu** button ▼ and choose **Start After Previous**.

53. One at a time, click each remaining item and set it to **Start After Previous**.

Add a Sound Effect to an Animation

54. Click the last item in the Animation pane, click its **menu** button ▼, and choose **Effect Options**.

55. Set the sound effect to **Applause** and then click **OK**.

56. Close the Animation pane.

57. Choose **Slide Show→Start Slide Show→From Beginning** and click each slide to view the presentation. Return to **Normal** view when you are finished.

58. Save the changes and then exit PowerPoint.

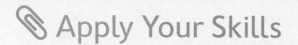 Apply Your Skills

---

APPLY YOUR SKILLS: P3-A1

Work with Pictures

In this exercise, you will add pictures and remove the backgrounds for the Universal Corporate Events presentation. You will also format the pictures to enhance the slides' visual appeal.

1. Start PowerPoint, open **P3-A1-UniversalPics** from the **PowerPoint Chapter 3** folder, and save it as **P3-A1-UniversalPicsRevised**.
2. Choose the **Catering** slide (third slide) and apply the **Two Content layout**.
3. Apply the **Two Content** layout to slides 4–9.
4. Display slide 3.
5. Click the **Online Pictures** icon, and then search for and insert a picture appropriate for a catering slide.
6. Search for and insert an appropriate photograph on slides 4–9. Each slide's photograph should represent the slide's text content.

Format Objects and Finalize the Presentation

7. Resize and reposition the photographs on each slide so they fill the right half of the slide.
8. Add a picture style or picture effect to each photograph. Use a maximum of two effect styles.
9. Remove each photo's background. You may want to resize or move the photos after removing the backgrounds.
10. Display the **Graphic Design** slide (fifth slide) and apply an artistic effect to the photo.
11. Save the changes and exit PowerPoint.

APPLY YOUR SKILLS: P3-A2

Add Shapes and Animations

In this exercise, you will add shapes and an animation to emphasize specific slides.

1. Start PowerPoint, open **P3-A2-UniversalAnimated** from the **PowerPoint Chapter 3** folder, and save it as **P3-A2-UniversalAnimatedRevised**.
2. Display the **Vegan** slide (third slide).
3. Insert the **Explosion 1** shape.
4. Type **Certified Vegan!** in the shape.
5. Resize and reposition the shape so it fills the area below the text.
6. Enlarge the font size of the shape's text to be as large as possible while remaining inside the shape.
7. Add the **Explosion 2** shape to slide 4 with the text **Certified Kosher!**
8. Resize and reposition the shape so it fills the area below the text.
9. Enlarge the font size of the shape's text to be as large as possible while remaining inside the shape.

10. Add the **Up Ribbon** shape to slide 5 with the text `Certified Organic!`

11. Resize and reposition the shape so it fills the area below the text.

12. Enlarge the font size of the shape's text to be as large as possible while remaining inside the shape.

Merge and Format Shapes

13. Display the last slide.

14. Insert a **Rectangle** shape and resize it so it is tall and thin.

15. Insert a **Teardrop** shape and adjust the size and shape so it looks like a candle flame. Position it on top of the thin rectangle.

16. Merge the **Rectangle** and **Teardrop** shapes into a single candle shape.

17. Copy the new candle shape and paste three copies on the slide, arranging them similarly to the following figure.

18. Go to **Shape Styles→Presets** and apply the **Gradient Fill – Dark Red, Accent 2, No Outline** style to the shapes on slides 3–6.

Apply Transition Effects and Animations

19. Select all slides but the title slide.

20. Apply the **Checkerboard** transition and set the Effect Options to **From Top**.

21. Display the second slide, *Catering*.

22. Apply the **Fade** animation to the bulleted paragraphs.

23. Use the Animation pane to select the *Kosher Dishes* item and set it to **Start with Previous**.

24. Set *Meat-lovers dishes* and *Desserts* to **Start with Previous** so that all four paragraphs will fade in at the same time after a click.

Add a Sound Effect to an Animation

25. Select the *Vegan dishes* item in the Animation pane and apply the **Applause** sound effect.

26. Close the Animation pane.

27. Choose **Slide Show→Start Slide Show→From Beginning** and click each slide until the slide show ends and you return to Normal view.

28. Save the changes and exit PowerPoint.

Add Visual Interest

In this exercise, you will add pictures, shapes, and animation to enhance the Universal Corporate Events presentation.

1. Start PowerPoint, open **P3-A3-UniversalVisual** from the **PowerPoint Chapter 3** folder, and save it as **P3-A3-UniversalVisualRevised**.

2. Display the second slide and change its layout to **Two Content**.

3. Use the **Online Pictures** icon on the slide to search Bing and insert a photo of a bus.

4. Use the Ribbon to open the **Insert Pictures** dialog box, search Bing for a photo of a limousine and a photo of a ferry boat, and add them to the slide.

5. Resize and position the three images on the slide to your liking.

6. Apply a picture style to each picture. Use the same style on all three pictures to maintain consistency.

Remove a Background and Apply Artistic Effects

7. Display the title slide.

8. Insert the **P3-A3-Hand.jpg** picture from the **PowerPoint Chapter 3** folder.

9. Use the **Background Removal** tool to remove the picture's white background.

10. Move the picture to the lower-right corner of the slide and resize it so it doesn't overlap any text.

11. Apply the **Photocopy** artistic effect to the picture.

12. Use the **Picture Tools→Format→Adjust→Color** gallery to apply **Color Tone→ Temperature: 7200k**.

Add, Merge, and Format Shapes

13. On the third slide, draw a wide **Rounded Rectangle**, a small **Rounded Rectangle**, and two **Circles**; arrange them into the shape of a bus.

14. Merge the shapes into a single bus shape.

15. On the fourth slide, use the **Rectangle**, **Oval**, **Right Triangle**, and **Manual Operation** shapes to create a limousine.

The Manual Operation shape is in the Flowchart category.

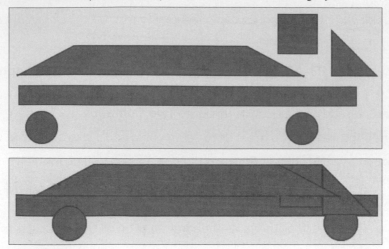

16. Merge the shapes into a single shape.
17. On the fifth slide, use the **Rectangle** and **Manual Operation** shapes to create a ferry boat.

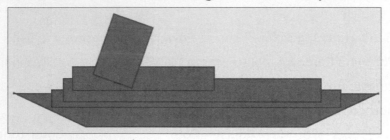

18. Merge the shapes into a single shape.
19. Apply the **Shape Styles**→**Theme Styles**→**Intense Effect – Green, Accent 4** style to each of the shapes on slides 3–5.
20. Resize and position the shapes so they fill the maximum area of their slides without overlapping the text.

Apply Transition Effects and Add Animation

21. Apply the **Reveal** transition to all but the title slide.
22. Set the effect on all slides to **Through Black from Right**.
23. Set the animation duration on all slides to **3** seconds.
24. Apply the **Fly In** animation to the hand picture on the title slide.
25. Set the option effect to appear **From Right**.

Use the Animation Pane to Add Sound

26. Use the **Animation** pane to add the **Whoosh** sound effect to the hand's animation.
27. Close the Animation pane.
28. Choose **Slide Show**→**Start Slide Show**→**From Beginning** and click each slide to view the presentation, returning to **Normal** view when you are finished.
29. Save the changes and exit PowerPoint.

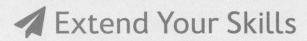# Extend Your Skills

These exercises challenge you to think critically and apply your new skills. You will be evaluated on your ability to follow directions, completeness, creativity, and the use of proper grammar and mechanics. Save files to your chapter folder. Submit assignments as directed.

P3-E1 That's the Way I See It

New PowerPoint users often use too many transitions, animations, and sound effects. In this exercise, you will see how less can be more. Create a new presentation, saved as **P3-E1-AnimationOverkill** and that includes at least six slides, in which every slide except the title slide includes a title, text, and an image. Apply any design theme and variation. Make sure the presentation focuses on a single idea (for example, a classic car collection, your favorite movies, or inspirational people). Apply a different transition to each slide. Apply a different animation to each text block and each image. Add a different sound effect to each slide. In other words—overdo it! View the presentation as a slide show.

Now save the presentation as **P3-E1-AnimationAppropriate**. Edit the presentation so each slide uses the same subtle transition. Remove the animation from each image and standardize the animation on the text blocks. Choose a subtle Entrance animation. Remove all sound effects. Save your changes. View the revised presentation as a slide show and compare it with your "overkill" version.

P3-E2 Be Your Own Boss

In this exercise, you will edit the animation on the Blue Jean Landscaping presentation. Open **P3-E2-BlueJeanAnimated** and save it as **P3-E2-BlueJeanAnimatedRevised**. View the presentation as a slide show and notice where the animations occur. Edit the presentation so the animations occur when a slide is clicked rather than automatically. Also, make sure the bulleted text animates one line at a time. Add a final slide using the Section Header layout. Use the title **Get Outside More** and the subtitle **It'll do you good!** Insert **P3-E2-Flowers.jpg** and make these changes:

- Remove the photo background.
- Move the image to appear behind the text.
- Apply an adjustment to make it less distracting.
- Apply the same slide transition used by the other slides.
- Add a sound effect that you feel is appropriate.

P3-E3 Demonstrate Proficiency

Stormy BBQ needs a slideshow to play on television screens throughout its seating area. It should feature images of mouth-watering barbeque. Create a new presentation named **P3-E3-BBQSlideShow**. Use at least five slides, where each slide includes a single photo of delicious barbeque. Remove the backgrounds from the images as necessary. Use slide transitions to fade one slide into the next. Include an animated title on each slide that names the dish. Choose one slide on which to add a shape. Add a shape from the Stars and Banners category with the text **Blue Ribbon Winner**. Format the shape and its text to add visual interest while keeping the text easy to read.

4 | Adding Multimedia to Presentations

Sound and movies can enhance a slide show to the point that a presentation is more than just information—it's entertaining. PowerPoint makes the development of "infotaining" presentations quick and easy. In this chapter, you will work with PowerPoint's media features to enhance your presentations.

LEARNING OBJECTIVES

▸ Acquire and add audio to a presentation

▸ Acquire and add video to a presentation

▸ Edit movies and add movie effects

▸ Use slide show timings

▸ Loop a presentation endlessly

Project: Adding Multimedia to the Presentation

iJam annually donates to a variety of charities, including animal rescue charities and young musician scholarships. You have been charged with creating a few new presentations that will play in a kiosk in the lobby at iJam's main office. They will showcase the animals and young musicians who have benefited from iJam's generosity. You want the presentations to be entertaining and engaging, but you also need them to run by themselves with no human physically clicking through the slides. You decide to add audio and video to the presentations and to use slide timings so that each presentation will run unattended.

Working with Multimedia

Multimedia, also called rich media, includes video and audio that can enhance a presentation. A photographer delivering a presentation may play a soundtrack of classical music while the slides display a gallery of wedding photos. A presentation used to train employees may have a spoken narration playing throughout the slide show to explain company policy. A summer camp director giving a presentation to prospective families may include videos of camp activities. Multimedia may be incorporated so simply as to play an audible click when navigating to subsequent slides during a presentation. Although multimedia can add excitement to your presentation, it can become over-whelming and distracting if used in excess.

 Add multimedia sparingly and only when there is true value in doing so.

Types of Multimedia

PowerPoint lets you add a variety of multimedia types to your presentation, including the following:

▸ Audio: This includes short sound effects such as a click or creaking door, as well as entire songs or narration soundtracks. Most users will be familiar with MP3 or WAV sound files.

▸ Video: This can include home movies from your smartphone, a camcorder, or downloaded videos from the Internet. PowerPoint does not let you create the video itself. You will need to create your video file in advance.

Linked Media Files

Most multimedia files exist as separate files that are saved outside your presentation but that are linked to it. However, when a linked multimedia file is moved or renamed, it will not play during the presentation. Therefore, it is recommended that you store the presentation and all linked media files in the same folder—and don't change the names of the multimedia files after they have been linked. Then you can easily copy all the files in the presentation folder to other media, such as a USB drive or CD, to share with people.

Organizing Media with Subfolders

If you have many linked multimedia files, you may decide to keep your files organized in subfolders rather than having all your files at the same level within a single folder. This makes it easier to find and launch your presentation and find any multimedia files you may need to edit.

Baby Laughing	intro sound
live band	Multimedia Presentation
narration 1	narration 2
New Method	time lapse

When all files are in the same folder, finding the one you need may be difficult.

Audio   Video   Multimedia Presentation

Organizing your files by type in subfolders makes it easy to find what you want when you want it.

DEVELOP YOUR SKILLS: P4-D1

In this exercise, you will create folders in which to store your various types of multimedia files.

1. Close all programs and folder windows so that only your Windows 10 Desktop is showing.
2. Click the **File Explorer** icon on the Windows taskbar and then maximize the **File Explorer** window.
3. Navigate to the **PowerPoint Chapter 4** folder and choose **View→Layout→Medium Icons**.
4. Choose **Home→New→New Folder**.
5. Type **Audio** as the folder name and tap [Enter].
6. Repeat steps 4–5 to create a second folder named **Video**.
7. Click the **P4-A1-TransportationNarration.mp3** file to select it.
8. Hold down [Ctrl] as you click these files to add them to the selection:
   - **P4-A3-Invites.mp3**
   - **P4-D2-bach-bwv813.mp3**
   - **P4-R1-Castle.mp3**
   - **P4-R1-Cheer.wav**
   - **P4-R1-Library.mp3**
   - **P4-R1-Lunch.mp3**
   - **P4-R1-Makeup.mp3**
   - **P4-R3-AudioBenefits.mp3**
9. After all nine audio files have been selected, release [Ctrl].
10. Drag any one of the selected audio files onto the **Audio** folder to move all nine selected files into that folder.
11. Click the **P4-A2-Band.mp4** file to select it.
12. Hold down [Ctrl] as you click these files to add them to the selection:
    - **P4-D7-Classical.mpg**
    - **P4-R2-ZeroPower.mp4**
    - **P4-R3-Video.mp4**
13. After all four video files have been selected, release [Ctrl].
14. Drag any one of the selected video files onto the **Video** folder to move all four selected files into that folder.
15. Close the folder window.

    Your chapter folder is now organized with multimedia subfolders.

Using Audio in Presentations

You have many options for acquiring audio to use in a presentation. Popular sources include the following:

▸ Searching for audio on your computer with the Audio on My PC command on the PowerPoint Ribbon

▸ Ripping audio from a CD

▸ Downloading an audio file from the Internet

▸ Recording your own narration directly in PowerPoint or with your own software

 Previous versions of PowerPoint came with a library of sound clips and access to more audio clips via the Microsoft Clip Art Gallery. These options are no longer available.

Audio File Types

Only audio files with a file type supported by PowerPoint may be added to a presentation. There are many types of audio formats, and PowerPoint supports the most popular ones. The following table lists the file types you can insert into a presentation.

SUPPORTED AUDIO FILE TYPES		
File Type	**Filename Extension**	**When to Use**
AIFF audio file	.aiff	Use as an alternative to WAV.
AU audio file	.au	
MIDI file	.mid, .midi	Use when computerized reproductions of instrumental music are desired.
		Use when instrumental music is needed and small file size is important.
MP3 audio file	.mp3	Use for music ripped from a CD or recorded narration.
Windows Media audio file	.wma	Example: A song that plays across slides throughout the entire presentation.
Advanced Audio Coding—MPEG-4 audio file	.m4a, .mp4	Use as an alternative to MP3.
Windows audio file	.wav	Use for small sound bites that are a few kilobytes in size.
		Example: A click sound or door-slam effect.

Adding Audio to a Presentation

Adding audio to a slide places a small speaker icon on the slide. This icon can be hidden from view during a slide show, or it can function as a start/stop button for the sound. When you insert audio onto a slide, you have the option to play the sound automatically after the slide loads or when you click the audio icon on the slide.

Inserting and Linking

Audio files can be either inserted (embedded) or linked. When inserted, the audio file is embedded in and becomes absorbed by the presentation file, causing the size of the presentation file to increase. When linked, it remains a separate file and does not increase the file size of the presentation. The following table compares the pros and cons of each method.

INSERTING VS. LINKING

	Inserting	Linking
Increases file size of presentation	Yes	No
Can move, rename, or delete audio file without breaking the presentation	Yes	No
Audio file size limit	Must be under 100 KB	Unlimited size

A slide with a speaker icon, indicating audio has been added to the slide

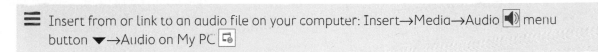

Insert from or link to an audio file on your computer: Insert→Media→Audio 🔊 menu button ▼→Audio on My PC 🔊

DEVELOP YOUR SKILLS: P4-D2

In this exercise, you will insert an audio clip from your computer. You must have speakers connected to the computer with the volume turned up to hear the audio.

1. Start PowerPoint and make sure the app window is maximized.
2. Open **P4-D2-Beneficiaries** from the **PowerPoint Chapter 4** folder and save it as **P4-D2-BeneficiariesRevised**.
3. Choose **Insert→Media→Audio menu button ▼→Audio on My PC**.
4. Navigate to your **PowerPoint Chapter 4\Audio** folder, select **P4-D2-bach-bwv813.mp3**, and click **Insert**.

   Remember that your computer may be configured to hide the file extensions and the .mp3 portion of the filename may not be displayed. The Insert command embeds the audio file into the presentation.

5. Drag the speaker icon to the top of the slide so that nothing overlaps the text.
6. Choose **Slide Show→Start Slide Show→From Beginning**.

   The sound does not play because it is configured to start playing On Click.

7. Move your mouse until the white mouse pointer arrow appears.

8. Move your mouse pointer over the speaker icon so the mouse pointer turns into a pointing finger and then click the speaker icon on the slide.

The sound starts playing.

9. Tap ⌊Esc⌋ to end the slide show.

10. Save your presentation.

Acquiring More Audio

Copying music from a CD into a digital music file on your computer is referred to as and can be accomplished with software such as Windows Media Player or the free Audiograbber (http://www.audiograbber.org). Windows Media Player rips to the WMA format by default but can rip to MP3 by installing a plug-in. Audiograbber is great in that it rips directly to MP3 with no additional configuration or plug-ins, so your ripped files are already in an appropriate format to use in a presentation—and a universal format to be played outside of your presentation. Be sure you are not violating any copyright laws if ripping sound from a CD.

Downloading Sound Effects

Many websites offer audio downloads in the form of sound effect clips, music background tracks, or promotional releases for bands. Again, be aware of copyright laws when downloading sound files.

Recording a Narration

If your computer has a microphone, you can record your own narration directly from PowerPoint.

≡ Insert→Media→Audio 🔊 menu button ▼→Record Audio

Choosing an Audio File Format

Whether you decide to download, purchase, rip, or record audio, you'll need to decide on the file format. Should you use a WAV file? A WMA file? An MP3 file? A MIDI file? What about AIFF or AU? Because WAV and MP3 files are the most prevalent, and every modern PC can play these without additional software or codecs, you should stick to these two file types when ripping or recording your own narration.

MP3 Compared with WAV File Format

If the files are only a few kilobytes in size, it doesn't matter whether you use WAV or MP3. However, MP3 files are compressed, whereas WAV files are not. Although WAV files may sound a little better to the trained ear, an MP3 of the same sound will be about one-tenth of the file size. Most people can't tell any difference in quality between a WAV and MP3. The MP3 encoding process attempts to remove audio information that is outside the range of what humans can hear. In other words, the average person won't miss the audio that was removed from an MP3 file but will certainly notice the smaller file size.

Dancing Queen.mid
MIDI Sequence
77.3 KB

 Dancing Queen.mp3
MP3 File
3.54 MB

 Dancing Queen.wav
WAV File
39.0 MB

Displayed is the same song saved as a 77.3 KB MIDI file, a 3.54 MB MP3 file, and a 39 MB WAV file. Note that the icons for the file types may differ from computer to computer based on personalized settings.

WMA File Format

The WMA format is an alternative to MP3 with comparable compression and quality, but not all music player software and hardware support the WMA format.

 Because the MP3 format is more universally supported, it is recommended over the WMA format.

MIDI File Format

MIDI files also have their place and are probably the third type of sound file you are likely to use. MIDI files don't contain sound information like WAV or MP3 files. They simply provide instructions to the computer to reproduce the sounds of musical instruments. What you hear when you play a MIDI file depends on your computer's sound hardware. Your computer may really sound like a violin when you play that MIDI file of a Paganini violin concerto, whereas another computer will not sound like a true violin at all.

 MIDI files cannot reproduce vocal tracks and should be used only when instrumental music is desired. (They are great for karaoke!)

Configuring Audio Options

When you add audio to a slide, you can choose to play the audio automatically or when clicked. If you choose to play the audio automatically, there is little reason to display the speaker icon on the slide because you no longer need to click it to play the audio. PowerPoint lets you hide the speaker icon in addition to setting a few more options.

 View the video "Audio Options."

Configuring Audio Styles

PowerPoint includes two Audio Styles shortcut buttons that automatically set audio options. These buttons are simply time-savers that set options for you in one click.

CONFIGURING AUDIO STYLES	
Button	**Settings Made Automatically**
No Style 🔊	• Start is set to On Click • Play Across Slides is disabled • Loop Until Stopped is disabled • Hide During Show is disabled
Play in Background 🔊	• Start is set to Automatically • Play Across Slides is enabled • Loop Until Stopped is enabled • Hide During Show is enabled

In this exercise, you will configure the sound to play automatically and hide the speaker icon.

1. Save the presentation as **P4-D3-BeneficiariesRevised**.
2. Click the speaker icon on the slide.
3. Choose **Audio Tools→Playback→Audio Options** and set the Start option to **Automatically**.

This option will start playing the audio automatically when the slide loads during the slide show. Because the sound will start automatically, there is no reason to display the speaker icon during the slide show.

4. Choose **Audio Tools→Playback→Audio Options** and place a check in the **Hide During Show** box.
5. Choose **Slide Show→Start Slide Show→From Beginning**.

   The speaker icon is hidden, and the sound starts to play immediately after the slide loads.

6. Move your mouse until the white mouse pointer arrow appears and notice that the speaker icon does not appear.
7. Click anywhere on the slide to advance to the next slide.

   The audio stops when the presentation advances to the next slide.

8. Tap [Esc] to end the slide show and return to Normal view.
9. Save your presentation.

Linking Audio

Linking media files instead of embedding them keeps the file size of the presentation smaller, which is good if you need to email the presentation to someone. However, the linked media must remain in the same location (the same folder) relative to the PowerPoint file, or the presentation won't be able to find the media to play it during a slide show.

Whether you choose to embed or link media is largely personal preference. While linking maintains a smaller presentation, embedding is often less problematic.

In this exercise, you will determine whether a sound is embedded or linked. You will then purposefully break the link to a linked file to see what happens when you attempt to play the presentation. Finally, you will repair the link and confirm that the media file plays.

1. Save the presentation as **P4-D4-BeneficiariesRevised**.
2. Choose **File→Info**.

3. Locate the *Related Documents* section at the bottom of the right column of Backstage view and note the absence of a link to Related Documents.

On the left, Edit Links to Files is not displayed, indicating no linked files. If there were linked files, Edit Links to Files would be displayed (as shown on the right).

4. Click **Back** ⬅ to exit Backstage view.

5. If necessary, choose the first slide from the slides panel.

6. Click the speaker icon on the slide and tap [Delete] to delete the embedded audio file.

7. Choose **Insert→Media→Audio menu button ▼→Audio on My PC**.

8. Browse to your **PowerPoint Chapter 4\Audio** folder.

9. Follow these steps to link to, rather than embed, the audio file:

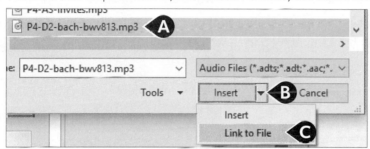

Ⓐ Click once on **P4-D2-bach-bwv813.mp3**.

Ⓑ Click the **Insert menu** button ▼.

Ⓒ Choose **Link to File**. The audio file is linked and is set to play On Click by default.

10. Drag the speaker icon to the top of the slide so it doesn't overlap any text.

11. Choose **File→Info**.

12. Locate the *Related Documents* section at the bottom of the right column of Backstage view and notice that the *Edit Links to Files* link exists, indicating there are now linked files.

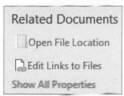

13. Click **Back** ⬅ to exit Backstage view.

14. Choose **Slide Show→Start Slide Show→From Beginning**.

15. Move your mouse until the mouse pointer white arrow appears.

16. Point at the speaker icon on the slide and then click the **Play** button on the control bar.

The audio file plays.

17. Tap [Esc] to end the slide show and return to Normal view.

Break the Link

18. Minimize PowerPoint.

19. Navigate to your **PowerPoint Chapter 4\Audio** folder and locate the **P4-D2-bach-bwv813.mp3** file.

If your computer is configured to display file extensions, the filename will be displayed as P4-D2-bach-bwv813.mp3. If your computer is configured to hide file extensions, the filename will be displayed as P4-D2-bach-bwv813 without any file extension.

20. Right-click the **P4-D2-bach-bwv813.mp3** file and choose **Rename**.

21. Follow the appropriate instruction to rename the file:
- If the filename displays as P4-D2-bach-bwv813 (no file extension), rename the file **P4-D2-bach**.
- If the filename displays as P4-D2-bach-bwv813.mp3, rename the file **P4-D2-bach.mp3**, taking care not to delete or duplicate the *.mp3* filename extension.

22. Maximize PowerPoint and choose **Slide Show→Start Slide Show→From Beginning**.

23. Move your mouse until the mouse pointer white arrow appears.

24. Point at the speaker icon on the slide and then click the **Play** button on the control bar.

The audio file fails to play because the link to the file has been broken. The message Media Not Found appears in the progress bar.

25. Tap Esc to end the slide show and return to Normal view.

Repair the Link

26. Choose **File→Info** and click **Edit Links to Files**.

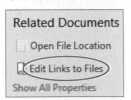

27. Click the link to **P4-D2-bach-bwv813.mp3** and then click **Change Source**.

28. Navigate to your **PowerPoint Chapter 4\Audio** folder, select **P4-D2-bach.mp3**, and click **Open**.

You have repaired the link. The Links dialog box displays the path to the source file you selected.

29. Click **Close** to close the Links dialog box.

30. Click **Back** ⊖ to exit Backstage view.

At the time of this writing, there is a bug in PowerPoint that causes the speaker icon on the slide to enlarge after repairing a link. If your speaker icon became larger, don't worry. It may look strange, but it will still work just fine.

31. Choose **Slide Show→Start Slide Show→From Beginning**.

32. Move your mouse until the mouse pointer white arrow appears.

33. Point at the speaker icon on the slide and then click the **Play** button on the control bar.

The sound plays because the link has been repaired.

34. Tap Esc to end the slide show and return to Normal view.

35. Save the presentation.

Creating Slide Show Timings

When using background music or a narration, you often want the slide show timed to the audio so the soundtrack and slides end at the same time. Rather than guessing when to advance to the next slide during a presentation, PowerPoint lets you automate the slide show by creating a slide show timing. You can even use slide show timings without audio to automatically navigate to subsequent slides during a live talk given by the presenter. As the speaker addresses the audience, the slide show can be on "autopilot," allowing the presenter to move away from the computer and interact more freely with the audience.

Determining Slide Timings

All it takes is a little math. If you can do simple division or have access to a calculator, you can time your presentation to your soundtrack and have both end at the same time. Assuming your audio begins on the first slide, and you want each slide displayed for an equal amount of time, follow these simple steps to determine the length of time to spend on each slide.

DETERMINING SLIDE TIMINGS

Goal	Steps
Determine the length of the audio file in seconds	• Select the audio icon on the slide. • Point at the right edge of the progress bar to see the total playing time of the audio file. • Convert this time to seconds. Example: A 2-minute and 30-second audio file would be 150 seconds.
Divide the total seconds by the total slides	• Use the Slides panel or Slide Sorter view to determine how many slides are in the presentation. • Divide the length of the audio in seconds by the total number of slides in the presentation. Example: A 150-second audio file used in a presentation containing 20 slides works out to $150 \div 20 = 7.5$
Determine the total time per slide	• If your division works out to a whole number, that is the number of seconds to spend on each slide. • If your division works out to a decimal, you'll have to round off or use another creative solution. Example: The answer to the division is 7.5. To apply this amount, you might display slide 1 for 7 seconds, slide 2 for 8 seconds, slide 3 for 7 seconds, slide 4 for 8 seconds, and so on.

Rehearsing Timings

PowerPoint's Rehearse Timings feature allows you to create an automated slide show. Use this feature to practice your speech and automatically have the slides advance as you speak, or time the presentation to a soundtrack so the audio ends just as the last slide appears.

≡ Create a slide show that runs automatically: Slide Show→Set Up→Rehearse Timings

≡ Slide Show→Set Up→Use Timings (check or uncheck)

DEVELOP YOUR SKILLS: P4-D5

In this exercise, you will configure the slide show to run by itself with a soundtrack.

1. Save the presentation as **P4-D5-BeneficiariesRevised**.
2. Select the speaker icon on the title slide and then choose **Audio Tools→Playback→Audio Styles→Play in Background** to automatically set the Audio Options.

   Several options in the Audio Options command group are automatically set: The speaker icon is hidden, and the sound will now start automatically. It will continue to play as you navigate through the slides and will start over again if it ends before the slide show.

3. Point at the right edge of the progress bar to determine the total playing time for the audio file.

   The sound is about 1 minute and 17 seconds (01:17) long.

4. Here's how you determine the number of seconds to allocate to each slide.

CALCULATING THE SLIDE TIMING	
General step	**In this case**
Determine the total number of slides in the presentation	10 slides
Determine the length of the sound clip in seconds	77 seconds
Divide the length of the sound by the total number of slides	77 ÷ 10
Round off	7.7 = about 7 or 8 seconds per slide

5. Locate the **Slide Show→Set Up** group.

   In the next step, you're going to use the Rehearse Timings feature. This is time sensitive because after you start the rehearsal, you're going to need to click the Next button every 7 or 8 seconds.

6. Click **Rehearse Timings** and click the **Next** button every 7 or 8 seconds until you reach the last slide.

7. Choose **Yes** when prompted to save your timings.

   If you make a mistake or want to start over, simply repeat steps 5–7.

8. Choose **Slide Show→Start Slide Show→From Beginning** and watch as the slide show auto-plays with the soundtrack. Click anywhere on the black screen after the slide show ends.

Loop a Slide Show

9. Choose **Slide Show→Set Up→Set Up Slide Show**.
10. Place a checkmark in the **Loop Continuously Until 'Esc'** option box and click **OK**.

11. Choose **Slide Show→Start Slide Show→From Beginning** and notice that when the last slide is reached (Corky), the slide show starts over again.

12. Tap ⎡Esc⎤ to end the slide show and return to Normal view.

13. Save and close your presentation.

Using Video in Presentations

Similar to audio, PowerPoint allows you to insert online video or a video file from your computer. Online videos include videos located on your Microsoft OneDrive cloud storage, YouTube, or other websites, provided you have the embed code.

Embed code is HTML code (web programming code) usually provided by the website on which the video is housed. If a website provides embed code for you to copy and paste, you can use it in PowerPoint. If the website does not provide embed code, you will not be able to use that video in PowerPoint.

 At the time of this writing, there is a bug in PowerPoint that prevents you from previewing videos from the Insert Video dialog's YouTube search results. If this happens to you, just use your web browser to search YouTube and then copy and paste the embed code into PowerPoint.

Using Online Videos

You must be careful when adding any kind of media— pictures, audio, or video—to a presentation. Not all media found with an Internet search is free to use. PowerPoint may let you search YouTube for media, but that's not a guarantee that you are legally allowed to use the media clip. It is safest to research the license of any media you want to use and then verify that it is in the public domain (free to use), royalty free (absent of royalty or license fees), or carries the Creative Commons license (free to use and share). Finding this information is not always easy and usually involves determining the owner of the media.

 At the time of this writing, PowerPoint supports embedding online videos only from YouTube.

Using Video from Your Computer

You can create your own full-motion video movie files by using the video camera built into a smart-phone and video-editing software such as the free Windows Movie Maker available for Windows or third-party software such as Studio made by Pinnacle (http://www.pinnaclesys.com). You can also download videos from the Internet. As with audio, you can either insert (embed) or link to a video. You indicate to PowerPoint whether you're linking or embedding by choosing the applicable option from the Insert menu within the Insert Video window.

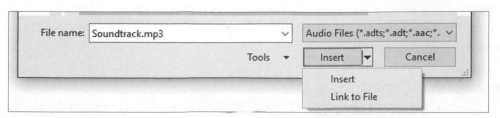

As with audio files, be sure you are not violating any copyright laws when downloading and using videos in a presentation. Always check a website's Terms and Conditions before using any downloaded multimedia content.

≡ Insert→Media→Video 🖳 menu button ▼→Video on My PC

Using Screen Recordings

New to PowerPoint 2016 is the ability to record video of your screen. This is helpful if you want to show a software demo or demonstrate how to use a particular website. Screen recordings are embedded in the presentation and are not saved as external files.

≡ Insert→Media→Screen Recording 🖳

≡ Windows + Shift + Q to stop recording

Video File Formats

Full-motion video, such as a home movie of your trip to the beach, manifests in several file formats such as MPEG or AVI. MPEG files are generally smaller files compared with AVIs and are less problematic when playing on different computers.

SUPPORTED VIDEO FILE TYPES

Video Format	File Extension
Windows media file	.asf
Windows video file	.avi
MP4 video file	.mp4, .m4v, .mov
Movie file	.mpg, .mpeg
Adobe Flash media	.swf
Windows Media Video file	.wmv

Codecs

Although you may think you're doing everything correctly by using a file with a supported file extension, your audio or video files may not play when the presentation is viewed on someone else's computer. This is most often due to a codec incompatibility.

The Role of Codecs

Audio and video multimedia files can be huge—sometimes several gigabytes. Software called a compressor is used to compress the file and make it smaller. To be played, the file must be decompressed or decoded—the job of more software called a decompressor. A codec, which is an abbreviation of compressor/decompressor, does both jobs.

If a multimedia file was created with a certain codec, that codec must be present on any computer wanting to successfully play the file. To confuse matters, many different codecs can create files with the same file extension, and they may not be compatible. For example, the I263, DivX, and Xvid codecs all create movie files with the .avi file extension.

Identifying a Codec

Don't assume that just because an AVI video file plays on your computer, it will also play on your friend's. Your computer may have the correct codec installed, while your friend's does not. This becomes an issue when using multimedia files compressed with codecs other than what Windows has installed by default—and is more of an issue with video than with audio. Software such as MediaInfo or AVIcodec—both free—can identify what codec is needed to play a certain video file.

Determining the Codec

You will find that AVI video files downloaded from the Internet may contain nonstandard codecs. Also, some digital video cameras create videos in nonstandard formats. The best advice is to simply try to play the video with Windows Media Player before inserting it in your presentation. If it plays in Windows Media Player, it will play in your presentation. If it fails to play, identify the codec by using software such as MediaInfo or AVIcodec. Then search the Internet for the codec, download it, and install it. The website VideoHelp.com is an excellent source for learning more about video and video codecs and offers a Tools section where you can download codecs and other helpful software.

 Make sure that your presentation computer has the necessary codecs for any movie to be played in your presentation.

DEVELOP YOUR SKILLS: P4-D6

In this exercise, you will add a video from an existing external file.

1. Open **P4-D6-Scholarship** from the **PowerPoint Chapter 4** folder and save it as **P4-D6-ScholarshipRevised**.
2. Choose **Home→Slides→New Slide** and type **Scholarship Recipient** as the title.
3. Click the **Insert Video** 🎞 icon on the slide and then click **Browse**.
4. Navigate to your **PowerPoint Chapter 4\Video** folder, select the **P4-D7-Classical.mpg** video movie file, and click **Insert**.

   Your computer may be configured to hide file extensions and may not display the .mpg portion of the filename. PowerPoint displays a message informing you that the video file must be optimized. A progress bar at the bottom of the PowerPoint window indicates the progress. Wait until the message box disappears.

5. Choose **Slide Show→Start Slide Show→From Beginning**.
6. Click anywhere to advance to the next slide.
7. Move your mouse around until the mouse pointer becomes visible.
8. Point at the video to display the control bar at the bottom and click the **Play** button.
9. Point at the video again to display the control bar and use the **Play/Pause** button to pause or resume the video.
10. When the video ends, tap [Esc] to return to Normal view.

    You may have heard a clicking sound at the beginning and end of the video—a sound the video camera itself made. Such sounds can be removed. You will do this later.

11. Save your presentation.

Editing Videos

PowerPoint offers the ability to edit videos. While PowerPoint is not meant to replace a full video-editing suite, it offers basic editing functions. You can trim the start and end of a video (cut off the beginning or the end) and have it fade in or out. You can edit audio the same way. Any audio or video editing you perform in PowerPoint has no effect on the actual media file. The editing affects only how PowerPoint plays the media; therefore, the edits are nondestructive.

 View the video "Trimming Videos."

☰ Video Tools→Playback→Editing

Applying Video Effects

PowerPoint also offers the ability to apply video styles. Using the Video Styles gallery, you can easily format a video much like pictures.

☰ Video Tools→Format→Video Styles

You can choose a predefined style from the Video Styles gallery or create your own custom effect by using the Video Shape, Video Border, or Video Effects menus.

Slides can be spiced up with a simple Video Style.

DEVELOP YOUR SKILLS: P4-D7

In this exercise, you will edit a video. You will then apply a Video Style.

1. Save the presentation as **P4-D7-ScholarshipRevised**.

2. Select the second slide, if necessary, and click the video to select it.

3. Choose **Video Tools→Playback→Editing→Trim Video**.

4. Ensure that your speakers are turned on and click the **Play** button. As soon as you hear the popping sound stop, click the **Pause** button.

The Play button turns into a Pause button while the video is playing.

5. If necessary, drag the blue playhead back to the start of the video and repeat step 4 until you can identify when the popping stops.

6. As the popping stops at about 1 second, drag the green trim control to the right until the number above it indicates that you are at about the 1-second mark. It doesn't have to be perfect, but should be close to 1 second.

The portion of the video to the left of the green trim marker is cut off.

7. Follow these steps to listen to the end of the video:

Ⓐ Click here toward the end of the video to set the playhead.

Ⓑ Click **Play** and listen for the pop. Notice that the pop occurs at the very end.

8. Follow these steps to trim the end of the video:

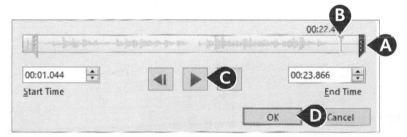

Ⓐ Drag the red trim control slightly left to cut off the portion of the video to its right.

Ⓑ Click here toward the end of the video and to the left of the red trim marker to set the playhead.

Ⓒ Click **Play** and listen for the pop to check if it has been removed.

Ⓓ If the pop is still audible, repeat steps A–C. When the pop has been removed, click **OK**.

Apply a Video Style

9. Choose **Video Tools→Format→Video Styles→More** 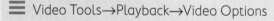 to display the Video Styles gallery.

10. Point at several styles to see them temporarily applied to the video on the slide and then choose **Intense→Monitor, Gray**.

11. Choose **Slide Show→Start Slide Show→From Current Slide**.

    The slide displays the video with the 3-D style.

12. Move your mouse until the mouse pointer white arrow appears.

13. Point at the video on the slide and then click **Play** on the control bar.

    The popping sounds at the beginning and end of the video are no longer heard because the video has been trimmed.

14. Tap ⌈Esc⌉ to exit the slide show and return to Normal view.

15. Save your presentation.

Setting Video Options

Just as with audio, there are several options you can apply to videos on a slide.

 View the video "Video Options."

≡ Video Tools→Playback→Video Options

There is no "wrong" or "right" when configuring these options. They are dependent on personal preference and the needs and expectations of the audience. For example, if your presentation were to play in a trade-show kiosk in a continuous loop to draw in a crowd, you would probably want video and audio to start automatically rather than requiring an icon to be clicked in order to start playback.

 At the time of this writing, there is a playback bug in PowerPoint. Even when set to play automatically, online videos from YouTube require you to click them to start.

In this exercise, you will configure a video to play in full-screen mode.

1. Save the presentation as **P4-D8-ScholarshipRevised**.

2. Select the **Scholarship Recipient** slide and then select the existing movie there, if necessary.

3. Choose **Video Tools**→**Playback**→**Video Options** and then click to place a checkmark in the **Play Full Screen** box.

4. Choose **Slide Show**→**Start Slide Show**→**From Beginning**.

5. Navigate to the second slide and move your mouse around until the pointer becomes visible.

6. Click the video to play it.

   The video plays in full-screen mode. When the video is done, it returns to normal size and the slide is visible again.

7. Tap Esc to end the slide show.

8. Save and close your presentation, and then exit PowerPoint.

Self-Assessment

Check your knowledge of this chapter's key concepts and skills using the Self-Assessment in your ebook or eLab course.

Reinforce Your Skills

Work with Audio

In this exercise, you will enhance a Kids for Change presentation that will be used at a high school assembly to recruit teens. You will add audio from your computer that needs to be edited and apply rehearsed timings so the slide show can run unattended.

1. Start PowerPoint, open **P4-R1-Tutoring** from your **PowerPoint Chapter 4** folder, and save it as **P4-R1-TutoringRevised**.

Embed Audio Clips from Your Computer

2. Display slide 1 and choose **Insert→Media→Audio menu button ▼→Audio on My PC**.

3. Browse to your **PowerPoint Chapter 4\Audio** folder, select **P4-R1-Cheer.wav**, and click **Insert**.

4. Drag the speaker icon to the top of the slide.

5. Display slide 4 and choose **Insert→Media→Audio menu button ▼→Audio on My PC**.

6. Browse to your **PowerPoint Chapter 4\Audio** folder, select **P4-R1-Lunch.mp3**, and click **Insert**.

7. Drag the speaker icon next to the word *Lunch*.

8. Choose **Insert→Media→Audio menu button ▼→Audio on My PC**.

9. Browse to your **PowerPoint Chapter 4\Audio** folder, select **P4-R1-Castle.mp3**, and click **Insert**.

10. Drag the speaker icon next to the word *Castle*.

11. Choose **Insert→Media→Audio menu button ▼→Audio on My PC**.

12. Browse to your **PowerPoint Chapter 4\Audio** folder, select **P4-R1-Makeup.mp3**, and click **Insert**.

13. Drag the speaker icon next to the word *Makeup*.

Link to an Audio Clip from Your Computer and Set Playback Options

14. Choose **Insert→Media→Audio menu button ▼→Audio on My PC**.

15. Browse to your **PowerPoint Chapter 4\Audio** folder, select the **P4-R1-Library.mp3** audio file, and click **Insert menu button ▼→Link to File**.

16. Drag the speaker icon next to the word *library*.

17. Display slide 1 and select the speaker icon on the slide.

18. Set the **Audio Tools→Playback→Audio Options→Start** option to **Automatically**.

19. Select the **Audio Tools→Playback→Audio Options→Hide During Show** checkbox.

Edit Audio

20. Display slide 4 and select the **Lunch** speaker icon.

21. Choose **Audio Tools→Playback→Editing→Trim Audio**.

22. Click **Play** and watch the blue playhead move across the sound wave. Notice when the English word *Lunch* is spoken and when the French word for *Lunch* ends.

23. Drag the green trim control to the right until it is just before the large bump in the sound wave (the start of the English pronunciation of *Lunch*).

24. Drag the red trim control to the left until it is just after the second large bump in the sound wave (the end of the French pronunciation of *Lunch*).

25. Click **OK**.

26. Click a blank area on the right side of the slide to deselect the speaker icon.

27. Trim the unwanted sounds from the beginning and end of the audio files on the remaining speaker icons.

Organize Media Files

28. Save your presentation and minimize PowerPoint.

29. Navigate to **PowerPoint Chapter 4\Audio** and create a new folder named **French**.

30. Drag these files into the **French** folder:
    - **P4-R1-Castle.mp3**
    - **P4-R1-Cheer.wav**
    - **P4-R1-Library.mp3**
    - **P4-R1-Lunch.mp3**
    - **P4-R1-Makeup.mp3**

31. Maximize PowerPoint and select the **Lunch** speaker icon on slide 4.

32. Click **Play** and notice that the audio plays because the **Lunch** audio file is embedded. Play the **Castle** and **Makeup** audio files, and notice that they also play.

33. Attempt to play the **Library** audio file. It fails to play because the link is broken.

34. Choose **File→Info→Edit Links to Files**.

35. Select the link to the **Library** file and click the **Change Source** button.

36. Browse to the **PowerPoint Chapter 4\Audio\French** folder, select the **P4-R1-Library.mp3** file, and click **Open**.

37. Close the Links dialog box.

38. Click the **Play** button and note that the **Library** audio now plays. If it doesn't, repair the broken link and, if necessary, trim the audio again.

39. Resize the Library speaker icon to match the others and trim the **Library** audio to remove the unwanted sounds from the beginning and end.

Apply Rehearsed Timings

40. Choose **Slide Show→Set Up→Rehearse Timings**.

41. When the timer reaches 5 seconds, click **Next**.

42. After the Math slide has displayed for 10 seconds, click **Next**.

43. After the Humanities slide has displayed for 15 seconds, click **Next**.

44. After the Language slide has displayed for 30 seconds, click **Next**.

45. Choose **Yes** to save the timings.

Run the Slide Show

46. Choose **Slide Show→Start Slide Show→From Beginning**.

47. Wait as the slide show runs automatically and displays the title slide for 5 seconds, the Math slide for 10 seconds, and the Humanities slide for 15 seconds.

48. When the Language slide appears, point to each speaker icon and click their **Play** buttons.

49. Tap Esc to end the slide show.

50. Save and close the file. Exit PowerPoint.

REINFORCE YOUR SKILLS: P4-R2

Work with Video

In this exercise, you will add video to a presentation for a Kids for Change parent meeting about math tutoring. You will also trim a video and apply video effects and playback options.

1. Start PowerPoint, open **P4-R2-Math** from your **PowerPoint Chapter 4** folder, and save it as **P4-R2-MathRevised**.

2. Display slide 2 and choose **Insert→Media→Video menu button** ▼**→Online Video**.

3. In the YouTube search box, type **Pythagorean theorem** and tap Enter.

Because of a bug in PowerPoint, you may not be able to preview the videos shown in the results. You may have to choose one based on the thumbnail and then play the video on the slide to see if you like it.

4. Select the thumbnail of your desired video and click **Insert**.

Insert an Online Video by Using Embed Code

Sometimes it is easier to browse and find a video directly from YouTube.

5. Display slide 3 and minimize PowerPoint.

6. Start Microsoft Edge, or the web browser of your choice, and navigate to **https://www .youtube.com**.

7. In the search box at the top of the web page, type **Fibonacci sequence** and tap Enter.

8. Click a video to watch it and continue previewing videos until you find one you like.

9. Once you find a video you like, click the **Share** link below the video.

10. Click the **Embed** link to show the embed code.

11. Tap Ctrl+C to copy the embed code.

12. Close your web browser and maximize PowerPoint.

13. Choose **Insert→Media→Video menu button** ▼**→Online Video**.

14. Click in the embed code box and tap Ctrl+V to paste the copied embed code.

15. Click the **Insert** menu button on the right side of the embed code box.

Insert a Video from Your Computer

16. Display slide 4 and choose **Insert→Media→Video menu button** ▼**→Video on My PC**.

17. Navigate to your **PowerPoint Chapter 4\Video** folder, select **P4-R2-ZeroPower.mp4**, and click **Insert**.

    Wait while PowerPoint imports and optimizes the video.

18. Save your presentation.

    You've completed a significant amount of work. This is a good time to save.

Edit and Style a Video

19. Click the video on slide 4 to select it, if necessary, and choose **Video Tools→Playback→ Editing→Trim Video**.

20. Click **Play** and listen to the cough at the beginning of the video.

21. Drag the green trim control to the right of the cough so the cough no longer plays (about 2 seconds from the beginning).

22. Click **Play** to verify that the cough no longer plays and adjust the green trim control if necessary.

23. Click **OK**.

24. Choose **Video Tools→Format→Video Styles→More** ▾**→Moderate→Compound Frame, Black**.

25. Apply the same video style to the videos on slides 2 and 3.

Set Video Playback Options

26. Display slide 4 and click the **video** on the slide to select it

27. Choose **Video Tools→Playback→Video Options→Start→Automatically**.

28. Save the presentation.

Run the Slide Show

29. Choose **Slide Show→Start Slide Show→From Beginning**.

30. Click the title slide to move to the Pythagorean Theorem slide.

    The video does not start to play because it is an online video.

31. Click the video to play it.

32. Tap Esc to stop the video, click the slide to move to the Fibonacci Sequence slide, and then click the video to play it.

33. Tap Esc to stop the video, and then click the slide to move to the Power of Zero slide.

    The video starts to play automatically because it was embedded from your computer.

34. Tap Esc two more times, once to stop the video and once to end the slide show.

35. Exit PowerPoint.

Work with Audio and Video

In this exercise, you will add audio and video to an automated Kids for Change membership drive presentation.

1. Start PowerPoint, open **P4-R3-AudioBenefits** from your **PowerPoint Chapter 4** folder, and save it as **P4-R3-AudioBenefitsRevised**.
2. Display slide 1, if necessary, and choose **Insert→Media→Audio menu button ▼→Audio on My PC**.
3. Navigate to the **PowerPoint Chapter 4\Audio** folder, select the **P4-R3-AudioBenefits.mp3** file, and choose **Insert menu button ▼→Link to File**.
4. Drag the speaker icon to the top of the slide.

Set Audio Playback Options and Edit Audio

5. Choose **Audio Tools→Playback→Audio Style→Play in Background** to automatically set the audio options.
6. Deselect the **Audio Tools→Playback→Audio Options→Loop until Stopped** checkbox.
7. Choose **Audio Tools→Playback→Editing→Trim Audio**.
8. Click **Play** and note when the speaker says, "Why should you join Kids for Change?"
9. Drag the green trim control to the right until it is just before "Why should you join Kids for Change?"
10. Click toward the right of the sound wave at about 01:00.000 to place the blue playhead toward the end of the file.
11. Click **Play** and note when the speaker says, "Ok, is that it?"
12. Drag the red trim control to the left until it is just before "Ok, is that it?"
13. Click **OK**.
14. Click **Play** on the slide and ensure that the audio begins with "Why should you join Kids for Change?" Also ensure that it ends with "The benefits are obvious." If necessary, trim the audio appropriately.

Organize Media Files

15. Save your presentation and minimize PowerPoint.
16. Navigate to your **PowerPoint Chapter 4** folder and create a new folder named **Benefits**.
17. Move **P4-R3-AudioBenefits.mp3** and **P4-R3-Video.mp4** into the **Benefits** folder.
18. Maximize PowerPoint and click the speaker icon on slide 1 to select it.
19. Click **Play** and notice that the audio fails to play because the link is broken.
20. Choose **File→Info→Edit Links to Files**.

21. Select the link to the **Benefits** file and click **Change Source**.

22. Browse to the **PowerPoint Chapter 4\Benefits** folder, select **P4-R3-AudioBenefits.mp3**, and click **Open**.

23. Close the Links dialog box.

24. Click **Play** and note that the audio now plays. If it doesn't, repair the broken link.

25. As necessary, trim the audio again now that the link has been repaired.

Apply Rehearsed Timings

26. Choose **Slide Show→Set Up→Rehearse Timings**.

27. Listen to the audio and click **Next** after you hear each of the following phrases:
    - "Why should you join Kids for Change? There are many benefits."
    - "...shows a college that you are not afraid to work for something worthwhile."
    - "...translates to effective management skills, which are important for any job applicant."
    - "...that you are willing to work hard to get the job done."
    - "Why should you join Kids for Change? The benefits are obvious."

28. Choose **Yes** to save the timings.

Run the Slide Show

29. Choose **Slide Show→Start Slide Show→From Beginning**.

30. Watch as the slide show runs automatically and the slides match up to the narration.

31. When the slide show ends, click the screen to return to Normal view.

32. If necessary, choose **Slide Show→Set Up→Rehearse Timings** and re-create the timings to match up better with the audio.

Insert a Video

33. Display the last slide and choose **Home→Slides→New Slide menu button ▼→Title and Content**.

34. Type **And It's Fun** us the slide title.

35. Click the **Insert Video** icon on the slide.

36. Choose **From a File→Browse**.

37. Browse to the **PowerPoint Chapter 4\Benefits** folder, select **P4-R3-Video.mp4**, and click **Insert**.

Edit and Style a Video

38. Choose **Video Tools→Playback→Editing→Trim Video**.

39. Click in the middle of the sound wave to place the blue playhead.

40. Drag the blue playhead to the right and note when the camera starts to move away from the girl, at about 12 seconds.

41. Drag the red trim control to the left to cut off the end of the video where the camera moves and then click **OK**.

42. Choose **Video Tools→Format→Video Styles→More →Intense→Reflected Bevel, White**.

Set Video Playback Options and Run the Slide Show

43. Choose **Video Tools→Playback→Video Options→Start→Automatically**.

44. Save the presentation.

45. Choose **Slide Show→Start Slide Show→From Beginning**.

46. Watch as the slide show plays automatically. When the last slide is displayed, the video should play automatically. When the video ends, tap Esc to end the slide show.

47. Exit PowerPoint.

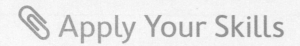

Apply Your Skills

APPLY YOUR SKILLS: P4-A1

Work with Audio

In this exercise, you will enhance a Universal Corporate Events sales pitch presentation. You will add audio from your computer that needs to be edited and apply rehearsed timings so the slide show can run unattended.

1. Start PowerPoint, open **P4-A1-Transportation** from your **PowerPoint Chapter 4** folder, and save it as **P4-A1-TransportationRevised**.

2. On slide 2, link to (don't embed) **P4-A1-TransportationNarration.mp3** from the **PowerPoint Chapter 4\Audio** folder.

3. Configure the audio on slide 2 to start **Automatically**, **Play Across Slides**, and **Hide During Show**.

4. Edit the audio on slide 2 to remove the noise from the beginning of the file.

Organize Media Files

5. Minimize PowerPoint and navigate to the **PowerPoint Chapter 4\Audio** folder.

6. Create a new folder named **Universal**.

7. Drag **P4-A1-TransportationNarration.mp3** into the **Universal** folder.

8. Maximize PowerPoint and attempt to play the audio file on slide 2.

9. Edit the link to the file so that the audio on slide 2 plays.

Apply Rehearsed Timings

10. Set up Rehearsed Timings so that slide 1 displays for **7 seconds** and each subsequent slide displays in time with the narration.

11. Choose **Slide Show→Set Up→Set Up Slide Show**, place a checkmark in the **Loop Continuously Until 'Esc'** option box, and click **OK**.

12. Save the presentation.

Run the Slide Show

13. Run the slide show and ensure that it plays automatically with slides timed to the narration.

14. Tap [Esc] to end the slide show.

15. Exit PowerPoint.

Work with Video

In this exercise, you will add videos to a presentation highlighting some of the entertainment services offered by Universal Corporate Events. You will also trim a video and apply video effects and playback options.

Insert Online Video

1. Start PowerPoint, open **P4-A2-Entertainment** from your **PowerPoint Chapter 4** folder, and save it as **P4-A2-EntertainmentRevised**.
2. Display slide 2 and click the **Insert Video** icon in the left placeholder.
3. Use the YouTube search box to search for and insert a video on **Line Dancing**.
4. Minimize PowerPoint and use your web browser to navigate to **http://www.youtube.com**.
5. Find another line-dancing video and copy the embed code.
6. Close the web browser and maximize PowerPoint.
7. Click the **Insert Video** icon in the right placeholder on the slide.
8. Paste the embed code into the proper box and click **Insert**.
9. If necessary, resize the videos so they do not overlap.

Add Video and Run the Slide Show

10. Display slide 3 and insert **P4-A2-Band.mp4** from the **PowerPoint Chapter 4\Video** folder.
11. Edit the video on slide 3 to remove the shaking at the beginning.
12. Apply the **Subtle→Simple Frame, White** video style to all three videos in the presentation.
13. Set the video on slide 3 to start **Automatically** and **Play Full Screen**.
14. Save the presentation.
15. Run the slide show and verify that the videos on slide 2 play when clicked and the video on slide 3 starts automatically at full screen.
16. Exit PowerPoint.

Work with Audio and Video

In this exercise, you will add audio and video to an automated presentation that will run in video kiosks of event venue lobbies.

1. Start PowerPoint, open **P4-A3-Invitations** from your **PowerPoint Chapter 4** folder, and save it as **P4-A3-InvitationsRevised**.

Add and Edit Audio

2. On slide 1, link to (don't embed) **P4-A3-Invites.mp3** from the **PowerPoint Chapter 4\Audio** folder.
3. Drag the speaker icon to the top-right corner of the slide.

4. Configure the audio clip to start **Automatically**, **Play Across Slides**, and **Hide During Show**.

5. Edit the linked audio clip to remove the noise from the beginning of the file.

Organize Media Files

6. Minimize PowerPoint and navigate to the **PowerPoint Chapter 4\Audio** folder on your file storage location.

7. Create a new folder named **Invitations**.

8. Drag **P4-A3-Invites.mp3** into the **Invitations** folder.

9. Maximize PowerPoint and attempt to play the linked audio file.

10. Edit the link to the file so that the linked audio file plays.

Apply Rehearsed Timings

11. Set up Rehearsed Timings so that each slide displays for about **4** seconds.

12. Run the slide show and ensure it plays automatically with sound. The narration should not get cut off at the end. If necessary, create new rehearsed timings to extend the length of the slide show.

13. Tap ⌐Esc⌐ to end the slide show.

Insert Online Video

14. Add a new slide to the end of the presentation by using the **Title and Content** layout.

15. Type **Celebrations** as the new slide's title.

16. Insert an Online Video and use the YouTube search to find a video on **Corporate Celebrations**.

17. Apply the **Intense→Perspective Shadow, White** video style.

18. Run the slide show and verify that the video plays when clicked. If it doesn't, delete it from the slide and try another online video.

19. Save and close the file. Exit PowerPoint.

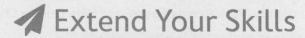 # Extend Your Skills

These exercises challenge you to think critically and apply your new skills. You will be evaluated on your ability to follow directions, completeness, creativity, and the use of proper grammar and mechanics. Save files to your chapter folder. Submit assignments as directed.

P4-E1 That's the Way I See It

You are creating a presentation to accompany your introduction to a group of campers you will be working with over the summer. You decide to share your favorite hobby in an effort to bond with your future campers. Create a blank presentation named **P4-E1-Hobby**. Change the first slide's layout to Title and Content. Title the first slide with the name of your favorite hobby (it could be sports, music, food, etc.) If you have access to a video camera (many smartphones have a built-in video camera), take a short video of yourself explaining your hobby. Transfer the video to your computer and then insert the video on the first slide. Edit it to trim off any unwanted beginnings or endings and apply a video style. Set it to play automatically. If you don't have a video camera, insert a clip art image depicting your hobby. Create a second slide and insert an online video depicting your hobby. Apply a video style and set the video to play when clicked. Add an appropriate slide title. Finally, apply a design theme.

P4-E2 Be Your Own Boss

You are creating an automated slide show highlighting gardens created by Blue Jean Landscaping. Open **P4-E2-BlueJean** and save it as **P4-E2-BlueJeanRevised**. Search the Internet and download an audio file to add to slide 1 appropriate for a garden slide show (e.g., light classical or cool jazz). Make sure the audio is legal to use. Set the audio to start automatically and ensure that it plays across all slides and loops until stopped. The speaker icon should not display during the slide show. Configure the slide show to run automatically, about 7 seconds per slide. Upon reaching the last slide, the slide show should automatically start over and loop continuously until [Esc] is pressed. Save and close the presentation.

Create a second presentation with four slides and save it as **P4-E2-HowTo**. On the title slide, add the title **Blue Jean Landscaping** and a subtitle of **How to Garden**. On each of the three remaining slides, use the YouTube search to insert an online video. Set each video to start when clicked. Add an appropriate title to each slide and apply a design theme to the presentation. Apply the same video style to each of the three videos so the presentation has a consistent look. Run the slide show and verify that each video plays. If a video fails to play, replace it.

P4-E3 Demonstrate Proficiency

To promote its cooking classes, Stormy BBQ wants to display a presentation on the restaurant television screens showing some of its favorite recipes. Create a blank presentation saved as **P4-E3-Recipes**. Add an appropriate title, subtitle, and design theme. Create a second slide using the Title and Content layout.

Use the Internet to find a YouTube video showing how to cook something appropriate for a barbeque restaurant. Copy the embed code from the YouTube page. Insert the video, using the embed code, to the second slide and add an appropriate title. Apply a Video Style and set the video to play when clicked. Search the Internet and download some public domain audio clips of people saying "mmmmm," "yummy," or making polite eating sounds. Add to slide 1. Set the audio to play automatically and hide the speaker icon during the slide show. Do not play the audio clips across all slides. Create Rehearsed Timings to display slide 1 for about 5 seconds, even if it cuts off the eating sounds. Make sure the timing for slide 2 is long enough to show the entire video.

Glossary

alignment Horizontal placement of text relative to the left and right margins of a cell or a page, where text is left-, right-, or center-aligned; or vertical placement of text relative to the top and bottom margins of a cell or page, where text is top-, middle-, or bottom-aligned

animations Special motion effects applied to individual objects on a slide, such as clip art or text

character spacing The horizontal space between characters

clip art Predrawn artwork that is added to computer documents

codec Software that compresses/decompresses sound and full motion video files; you must have the proper codec installed to play a sound or full-motion video

demote To increase text indentation so it appears farther away from the left margin and, if numbered or bulleted, reduces the numbering or bulleting level to the next lower level

embed To set a file, such as an Excel spreadsheet or another PowerPoint presentation, so it is absorbed into the current presentation; changes to an embedded file have no effect on the original object

footer Text that usually, but not always, is located toward the bottom of a document, slide, or handout and that repeats on all (desired) pages, slides, or handouts within a document or presentation

handout master Controls the format of handouts

handouts Printouts of slides for presentation attendees; can be used for note taking

header Text that usually, but not always, is located toward the top of a document, slide, or handout and that repeats on all (desired) pages, slides, or handouts within a document or presentation

justify Text alignment where character spacing is automatically adjusted differently for each line in the paragraph so the left and right side of the paragraph form straight lines

kerning The horizontal space between pairs of characters; *see* character spacing

line spacing Vertical space between lines of text

linked (object) Object created in a source file and inserted in a presentation; object retains a link to the source file; destination file can be updated when source file is modified

multimedia Audio or video that enhance a presentation; also called *rich media*

Outline panel Located on the left side of the screen; displays the text content of each slide

promote To reduce text indentation so it appears closer to the left margin and, if numbered or bulleted, to elevate the item to the next higher level of bullet

Rehearse Timings Feature that automates the advancement of slides during a slide show by defining the number of seconds to stay on each slide, using the Slide Show→Set Up→Rehearse Timings command creates slide show timings

Ribbon Band at the top of an application window that contains the commands required to complete a task; organized in tabs that relate to a particular type of activity and groups of related commands (some tabs are only shown when needed, such as Chart Tools, Table Tools, or Picture Tools)

ripping Copying sound from an audio CD to your computer

sections Groups of slides treated as a single object, making it easy to change the order of large blocks of slides

slide layout Preset layout of placeholder boxes on a slide

slide show timing Automating the advancement of slides during a slide show by defining the number of seconds to stay on each slide; using the Slide Show→Set Up→Rehearse Timings command creates slide show timings

Slide Show toolbar Contains navigation controls, drawing tools, and options to be used during a slide show presentation; located in the bottom-left corner of a slide during a slide show

slide transition Animation that occurs when navigating from one slide to the next during a slide show

standard format Slide size with the ratio of 4:3

theme Preset formatting selections you can apply to a presentation; include colors, graphic elements, and fonts all designed to work well together and quickly achieve the look of a professional design; in PowerPoint, themes include matching backgrounds, placeholder positions, matching color schemes, and text formatting

tracking The horizontal space between a range of characters; *see* character spacing

widescreen format Slide size with the ratio of 16:9

Index

Note: Index entries ending in "V" indicate that a term is discussed in the video referenced on that page.

NOTES

NOTES

NOTES

NOTES

NOTES

NOTES